FROM CERTAIN DEATH TO SAVING LIVES

THE DAVID BARROWS STORY

Written by Melodye Faith Hathaway with David Barrows

DEDICATION

It is with difficulty I dedicate this book because there are so many who have walked this road with me, but I will try:

To my loving mother, Barbara Barrows, who never gave up on me, and stayed by my side no matter what;

To my six brothers: Johnny, Alan, Jeff, Mark (Charlo), Kevin, (KB) and Jimmy. I can't imagine my life without you all;

To my two growing sons, Bradley Adam and Hunter Jacob, I love you both so much;

To Tracy Rice who never gave up on me even when I had given up on myself;

To the one who has dedicated her life and her time to Hunter and me; the one who never gave up on me and refused to believe what the doctors said about my condition; the one with all the faith, Faith Kranenberg;

And, of course, to my Lord and Savior, Jesus Christ, who makes all things possible!!

DAVID'S FORWARD

Growing up as one of seven boys, I was nicknamed "Go-Go" for a reason… I was never slowing down and always willing to try new things. I didn't know exactly where I fit in so I just followed.

What I found at the end of my "Go-Go" years was death!

But, I was given a second chance at this thing we call LIFE.

Today I take nothing for granted. Each breath I take, each moment I spend with family and loved ones, each time I stand alone on my back porch to listen to Nature's sounds; all gifts from God. What treasures we all can find when we take a moment and realize someone does love us and cares NO MATTER WHAT.

Today I am grateful and not afraid to express what I think about living and loving life and what it is all about. Because without love what do we have?

We are never alone; all we need to understand is that God is real and if we follow His words He will see us through any trouble that may arise.

He has seen me through more trouble than most people can imagine.

I want to share here with you my unforgettable past life of trying to fit in somewhere by the use of drink, drugs, girls and an "anything goes" attitude.

By reliving my past life here, I only pray that I can touch even one still suffering alcoholic or drug addict from ever having to go through what I will carry the rest of my life; traumatic brain injury (T.B.I.), re-construction of my face, loss of feeling on the left side of my face, left arm, left leg, and the loss of eyesight in my left eye.

And, I ask you, my friends, to come along with me as I share the highs that led me further into the deepest darkness of my former self, as well as the rock-bottom lows that led to my destruction and death, and how I was destined to "Go-Go"

FROM CERTAIN DEATH TO SAVING LIVES!

David L. Barrows
February 14, 2015

THANK YOU!

HOW DO I SAY THANK YOU WITHOUT ALL MY EMOTIONS TAKING ME TO A PLACE IN MY HEART THAT TODAY FEELS EVERYTHING?

Sitting here writing this thank you section I'm crying my eyes out. As the tears hit the paper all I can think of is what you all gave up for me!

FIRST AND FOREMOST, I want to say thank you to the God I serve today who NEVER gave up on me and will forever be my best friend!

I would like to thank the mother and daughter paramedics from Slanesville, West Virginia. They were the first ones to work on me at the scene of my accident. And I want to thank the Augusta EMS Ambulance who also arrived at the scene of the accident to assist us.

I would like to thank the pilot and EMT team who flew me to the critical care hospital in Cumberland, Maryland.

To the entire staff at the Cumberland Memorial Hospital who worked on me in the critical care emergency room, thank you.

Thanks to Dr. Answano, the attending E.R. doctor who relentlessly worked on me to save my life.

Thank you to Dr. Villanuava and Dr. Palin who reconstructed my face at the Cumberland Memorial Hospital.

To all the nurses and other staff on the first and second floor of the Cumberland hospital, thank you. Dr. Sprenkle who was in charge of putting my life support on and off and who put in a chest tube when my lungs collapsed, thank you so much.

I would like to thank Dr. Biundo and everyone at Health South Rehabilitation Hospital in Morgantown, West Virginia where I was transported to after coming out of my coma.

Thank you to Micah Anthony, Michelle Henry, Amanda and Speech Therapist Tresa, as well as the entire therapy team, who never gave up on me and loved me when I couldn't love myself.

Thank you so much to Ruth and Ted Kranenberg for everything they have done to help me through recovering from this accident and finding a new way to live. Words simply cannot express what their loving kindnesses have meant to me.

Special thanks to The Professor, Tracy Rice, the woman who never left my side; never gave up on me when I gave up on myself! Tracy has been my ROCK through it all! She served as my foundation for healing and continues to be my steadfast compass that guides and drives me to be the best I can be...and, as one of my greatest friends, Tracy Rice has cried with me, walked with me and showed me the true meaning of WE CAN! She deserves an extra thank you "hug" as the greatest physical therapist who has become my hero!

Thanks to the entire nursing staff at Health South in Morgantown, West Virginia; oh how I kept these women on their feet caring for me!

Thank you to my mother, Barbara, and to Faith Ann Kranenberg, who never left my side through this entire miracle!

To all my brothers and family who never stopped visiting and praying for my healing, thank you from the bottom of my heart.

Thanks to Mark and Abby who were stronger than most when I was able to see my family.

To my hometown of Hampshire County, West Virginia who welcomed me back home with open arms, cards and letters.

Special thanks to the Eby family from Beans Cove, Pennsylvania for all their prayers and support during my hospitalization.

To my two sons, Bradley Adam and Hunter Jacob who I know their prayers were heard.

To Alligator Angie from the great state of Florida who re-introduced me to our God....Jesus loves us, Ang!!

Thanks to my friend, Anne Latch Benedict, who re-introduced me to the outside world after I came home from my accident recovery by taking me to see the Kix concert and my class reunion.

Thank you to Pastor Don Kesner and Christ Community Church for allowing me to share my story.

Thanks to all the schools in West Virginia who have me come speak to thousands of students each year.

I would like to thank the world's greatest best friends and buddies who kept in touch with me through our entire lives, through thick and thin and proved there are still great friendships!

Thank you to the Hott family in Augusta, West Virginia for being the world's greatest neighbors.

To all my Facebook family and friends who walked with me every step of my journey through brain damage, (T.B.I.), and across the world friendships, I wanted to say thank you...and, as the song title says: My God IS Unstoppable! Miracles Do Happen...David-

Thanks to Robert "The Bubbler" Boline and Robert "Sal" Salvini, my best friends growing up…together we were: "The 3 Musketeers".

I want to thank the organizations that have helped me be clean and sober over ten years now and counting: AA and NA. Through my God I have met the world's greatest recovery team at my home group in West Virginia. Rich A., Dave G., Marvin, Mike, George, Christine, Gail H., Laura, John Z., and, the leader, OUR GOD!

I want to give a special recognition to Cindy S. and Carol from my home group of AA. They have been my foundation in the recovery process!

Also, please forgive me for any omissions to this list as so many have rallied and helped me and my family in one way or another over the years. I may not have the names here, but thanks to everyone who have been involved in my life through the good times as well as the bad. You are all appreciated more than you will ever know!

Thanks to the writer of this book, who saw me through terrible memories of my past and reliving my miracle accident, and for showing me love still exists! Thanks Melodye Faith Hathaway…You are the BOMB!! LOL

Melodye and I have never met, but she has walked miles with me in spirit, reliving my painful past, crying with me, and sharing with me to understand my fears and joys!

Lastly, I want to say AGAIN thank you, God, for all YOU have done for me! You took a brain damaged, drug addicted, alcoholic, one eyed, reconstructed man and said,

"Hold My hand and WE will walk this road together, One day at a time…"

And, it is because of you, my GOD; I am clean and sober today. You have given me yet another chance to be my sons' daddy, to be a friend again to my friends, to be my brothers' brother. I can wave to my neighbors; I can call my best friends; I get to be a son to my mom; Faith's loving man, but most importantly, I can go outside and thank and praise my Unstoppable God!

THANKS for another day with YOU!

~David

"MY GOD IS UNSTOPPABLE"

FROM THE WRITER

What you are about to read is the true account of The David Barrows Story. I am proud to have been chosen to put pen in hand so he can give an account of this incredible story to the world as it should be told.

Even though David and I have never met in person, we have shed many tears together over the phone, through Facebook and in texts to get his message out through this book. I am so honored and it truly has been a labor of love for me to be chosen to help him bring his story out at this time and in this way to help others who are out there in this world, hurting, but may not have any idea how to get the help they are crying out for.

David has already saved many lives with his talks to area schools, correctional facilities, universities and more. I pray that his story will reach even more who desperately need to find a way to get off the path of destruction and back onto the right roads that will lead them to safety and recovery.

What you are about to read is David's account of how he has recovered FROM CERTAIN DEATH TO SAVING LIVES.

David shares with heartfelt, vivid details his fight with alcoholism, drug addiction, and more demons than many of us could ever imagine. This is not an easy thing for him to do, but he CHOOSES to do it in hopes it will save lives as his God has saved his.

First, and foremost, I want to take this opportunity to give you some information on places you can go for help if you or someone you know is hurting and needs guidance. The following are some suggestions of where someone may be able to get help like David has.

You can obtain information on help with alcoholism through an organization called Alcoholics Anonymous or AA. This is the website where they can be reached:

http://www.aa.org/

There is also a separate organization for help with drug addiction called Narcotics Anonymous or NA:

http://www.na.org/

There are local groups of both of these organizations in your surrounding area, or you may contact them through a local hospital or church to find out where and when they meet.

David has many permanent injuries he sustained from his ATV accident which you will be reading about in this story. Some of these injuries you can see if you look hard enough or if he points them out to you, but there are some you can never see. One of the unseen injuries David suffers is Traumatic Brain Injury which is usually shortened to T.B.I.

Traumatic Brain Injury is a major cause of disability and death in the United States today. T.B.I. survivors suffer effects lasting from a few days to the rest of their lives. It affects a person's thinking, their memory, their vision, their hearing as well as their movements and emotions. They also suffer personality changes and depression. T.B.I. affects not only the individual that suffers from it, but it can have lasting effects on their families, friends and work as well.

One of the most difficult things for sufferers of T.B.I. is that this is an invisible disability and undetected when someone meets the affected person. So many people have a difficult time understanding and grasping how it affects the survivor on a day-to-day basis.

T.B.I. happens when some type of external mechanical force causes brain dysfunction and is usually the result from an accident that creates a violent blow or jolt to the head. Any foreign object penetrating the skull, such as a bullet or shattered piece of skull, could also be the cause of it.

A mild form of T.B.I. can cause temporary dysfunction, but more serious T.B.I. is the cause of permanent physical damage to the brain and may result in long-term consequences. The impact on a T.B.I. sufferer and their family and friends can be devastating to say the least.

There are many sites on the Internet to educate and give support to caregivers, family, friends and survivors of T.B.I. These sites offer to help ease the transition from shock and despair at the time of the brain injury to coping and problem solving for these survivors and their loved ones.

Valuable information about the latest medical breakthroughs on research and up-to-date available treatment available for brain damage, as well as all symptoms resulting from brain injuries, along with the nation's best traumatic brain injury rehabilitation centers and resource information is available. This link may be of assistance to those who want to learn more about T.B.I.:

http://www.cdc.gov/traumaticbraininjury/get_the_facts.html

What David has found that helps him the most is being surrounded by other T.B.I. survivors with a support group at Morgantown, West Virginia and he is in the process of starting a T.B.I. support group at the local hospital in Augusta, West Virginia sometime in the near future.

Support groups are vital to recovering Alcoholics, recovering Drug Addicts and T.B.I. survivors.

David goes all over the state of West Virginia and beyond to schools teaching the children ATV (all-terrain vehicles) safety since his accident. He also does drug and alcohol awareness at high schools and universities as well as T.B.I. awareness.

The website on ATV safety, rules and regulations is:

http://www.cpsc.gov/en/Safety-Education/Safety-Education-Centers/ATV-Safety-Information-Center/

And, lastly, my hope is that everyone that reads David's story will be inspired by the West Virginia Miracle Man because...

MIRACLES DO HAPPEN!

Melodye Faith Hathaway
Author/Motivational Speaker
February 14, 2015

TABLE OF CONTENTS

INTRODUCTION

I hope you understand and I really want you to know what I'm about to write is the biggest truth I've ever lived.

I was touched by the hand of God and the hand of my mother. I was also touched by the hand of my father as he walked with me for a moment in Heaven.

I was given a gift so big I will never be able to repay so that is why this book is being written and I'll travel across this world to give in return what was freely given to me: a second chance at the thing we call life that so many take for granted.

Today I am outspoken about my accident and my recovery. But, first let me introduce you to the Barrows Family, Mom, Dad and seven boys!

Introductions can be tricky so just let me say that I could not have asked for a more loving family than the one I came from. We were and are the Barrows Family!

Today I travel where invited across the United States giving motivational and inspirational talks about the life I led and where it took me…to Death and back to Life for a second chance to save myself and many others who are just like me!

I am a T.B.I. survivor! I have 10 years and counting clean and sober! I have witnessed first-hand the power of my unstoppable God!

Most all of my talks start with A.T.V. Safety, Drug and Alcohol Awareness and living with Traumatic Brain Injury (T.B.I).

Impacting so many other peoples' lives it's amazing to me how I went from the life I led to now reaching out to you!

The clapping and cheering with tears falling from the faces of those I'm invited to share my story with is normally met with a standing ovation!

Crying myself as I stand before clubs, organizations, groups, churches and schools I often ask myself how I ever got to where I am now in my life. Do I deserve all of this clapping and cheering? Why do you want to take your picture with me or have my autograph in your book?

I've been called "The Miracle Man" and I am always in my hometown newspaper. My story has stayed local in West Virginia but it's time to now go global as my mind and body has healed enough to reach for your hand!

My name is David Barrows and may I ask you just one favor? Put everything you're doing away and let me tell you a little story of how I went FROM CERTAIN DEATH TO SAVING LIVES!

CHAPTER ONE:
IT'S TIME THE STORY IS TOLD

I grew up having the greatest childhood a kid could EVER ask for. In fact, I could not have dreamed of a better one.

Born in northeast Pennsylvania, my backyard was Lake Erie where I learned to swim, fish, and spend time with my brothers.

There were nine of us; I was the sixth of seven boys and had the greatest parents anyone could want.

My father, who owned and ran his own business, worked day and night to show us a life he never had. I remember never wanting for anything! We had every toy, the best clothes, lots of money, but the best thing we had was each other!

There was so much love in my home between us all and my mom also taught us about an even greater love from a man called God.

When I was nine years old, my father moved our family from northeast Pennsylvania to Chambersburg, Pennsylvania where he built a brand new home in Penn National Estates. It was a beautiful golf course community surrounded by breathtaking mountains and gorgeous streams.

The Fourteenth Green was our backyard...

I remember playing football on the golf course with all my brothers along with our neighborhood friends. There were lots of great times and we were always having fun.
My older brothers always invited me to come along in everything they were doing at the time. We enjoyed each other's company and stuck together whenever trouble would arrive. There were so many of us brothers some families didn't want to start any trouble with the knowledge we always had each other's backs.

Then there was the golf course at nighttime; I remember such fun times there. It seemed to be a meeting place for all my friends and me.

Right across from the 14th Fairway was the lake we swam in at night finding golf balls...me, my little brother, Jimmy, and my best friend, Rob the Bubbler. The three of us had so much good, clean fun.

We loved to take the golf carts and would ride them all through the course and enjoyed being chased by the golf course's night security.

My older brothers were always there when "Go-Go" (my nickname) got into trouble. I never had to fight any fight alone. I would start trouble with other boys knowing that my brothers would be there to back me up.

Johnny was the oldest son who was a standout in high school sports. He ran track and field and overshadowed most others when it came to football.

Johnny met and married, Barbie, the most beautiful girl in school who would become an anesthesiologist in North Carolina.

Barbie always liked me and I always felt safe and happy when she would take the time to talk and help me as I was growing up.

Johnny made All American in football and ended up playing semi-pro for the Chambersburg Cardinals and the Yellow Jackets.

He always wore the #9 jersey and still to this day I treasure the jersey he gave me after a game when I was the water boy for his team.

After football, Johnny retired and now resides in North Carolina where he and Barbie enjoy the Atlantic Ocean and their retirement.

Alan was the second in line and *was* and still *is* the brains of the bunch. He attended Gannon College where he learned about business and life. Alan, or A.B. as we called him, worked at Dad's business and eventually took over as Brother, Boss and Financial Advisor.

I remember buying my first new truck and Alan always made sure my payments were made and made on time! I loved that little blue Nissan truck that he helped me get and call my own.

Alan comes to my home in West Virginia to visit and spend time with me since my accident, always reminding me that my God is Unstoppable. He still loves me after all I've done, and tells me a pair of aces is a great hand in poker but it can be beat...

Brother Jeff, or as I call him, Jeff Bear, is the biggest Barrows boy. After returning home safely from the Army Jeffery worked at a huge army base in Chambersburg, Pennsylvania where he retired.

Jeffery is the greatest turkey caller and turkey call maker I know. He has a Turkey Beard collection that would make any hunter jealous.

Now onto the wildest Barrows boy, Mark Joseph, or as most people call him, Charlo! (Fish on!)

Mark was and still is the closest brother to me. We have done about everything together.

He was the first family member to arrive at the hospital where I laid dying in May, 2005, and was able to give the hospital permission to treat me. He and the Eby family prayed over me asking God to please save my life. Thank you also, Truman, Conrad and Durrell Eby!

Kevin Francis Barrows is next in line, but we all just call him K.B. He is quiet and shy and the most handsome Barrows boy with blonde hair, big muscles; a real ladies man.

He finally found his dream girl when he met Deb and now they do everything together; hunt, fish and travel the country.

Kevin is known to be the greatest deer and turkey hunter ever! He will climb up in his tree stand in the early morning hours before the sun comes up and stay until it goes down at dusk. He has a trophy room that any hunter would be jealous of and cigar boxes full of turkey beards!

Jimmy is the youngest Barrows boy, but by no means the smallest. Jimmy is a rock solid man and not afraid of anything. He has learned from each of his brothers and has all the qualities of every one of us. Jimmy learned to bow hunt from Brother Kevin and has taken over the role of Archery King. He now lives his life in Oklahoma with his woman, Sammy, and he has also become a great painter!

When I had my ATV accident Jimmy stayed at the hospital for weeks until he knew I was safely in God's hands.

One day in May, 2005, like always, the brothers rallied together and rushed to Cumberland Hospital in Maryland only to find their little brother, "Go-Go", so badly hurt the doctors didn't give them much hope for me.

I had been in a terrible ATV accident. After being pronounced dead three times and taken by life-flight to the nearest critical care hospital, the doctors had tried everything and told my family if I made it through the next twelve hours it would be nothing short of a miracle.

But…wait a minute, let me go back to my childhood because I made some decisions back then that led to the day I died and was given a second chance to come back and SAVE LIVES!

L to R: Cousin Jon Jon, David, K.B., Mark, Cousin Jody, Gramma Nick, Jeffery, Alan

CHAPTER TWO:
GROWING UP DAVID

The Leader of my family was my dad, Albert Harlow Barrows, a man among men. He grew up in Hancock, New York and never had much in his life other than his two brothers, Ivan and Howard.

My father couldn't wait until he turned 17 to enlist in the Navy and travel the world fighting in WWII. He never spoke much about his time there because, like so many other soldiers, he watched many of his military friends give their lives for this great country we live in today.

From time to time he would mention Okinawa or Iwo Jima. I could hear in his voice they were not good times. He told me one day when I was just a boy that he never even had a bicycle and he was going to see that his boys would never want for all the things he longed for as a kid. My dad made good on all his promises to himself and I can't ever remember wanting for anything.

He built a business and worked until he couldn't work anymore. In June of 2004 my dad was called Home to Heaven but it was not the last time I would hear, see or speak to him. Keep reading this book and you will read about my first gift from God.

My mother, "The Saint", Barbara Barrows was born and raised in Binghamton, New York where she had the most beautiful sisters, my Grandma "Nick" Edna Knickerboker and Rex to look over her.

I remember traveling to Binghamton, New York to visit my grandmother and grandfather and getting to meet all my aunts, uncles and cousins. My mother's sister, Aunt Judy, would become my godmother! I loved Uncle John's B.B.Q. cooking and have many fond memories playing with their children, Jon Jon, and Jody Baron. Today Jody and Jon Jon stay in touch with me through Facebook and family reunions.

Another sister of my mom's was Aunt Theresa and her husband was Uncle Don. I could write an entire book about this woman who raised my cousins, the Bailys. They had the most beautiful daughter, Karen, who was protected by the Baily Boys who were the wrestling champions of all of New York.

My mother put up with all her boys' shenanigans by introducing us to *the chair* in her kitchen and a man named Jesus!

Now, to this day, my brothers all are alive and well with whom I have an unbreakable bond with!

Like I said before, I was born in northeast Pennsylvania in 1963; the sixth of seven sons to Barbara and Albert Harlow Barrows. We lived right beside Lake Erie.

My story never really started though until I moved with my family when I was nine years old to Chambersburg, Pennsylvania. My father had a growing sales business along with seven growing boys.

So it was me and my six brothers, no sisters. I can recall always having a good time and always having someone to play with.

Life was so much fun growing up with all those boys.

My oldest brother was Johnny. He was a high school standout in sports. He ran track and football and dated the most beautiful girl in school, Barbie. He also was the greatest athlete in my family. He played semi-professional football for the Yellow Jackets, the Chambersburg Cardinals and he could outsell most all other salesman with the exception of my brother, Mark.

My brother, Alan, was the smart one, who to this day I call Mr. Commonsense, and ended up running my dad's business. Jeff went into the Army and returned to be a guard at a huge Army base. Mark worked for my dad, like me, and the youngest, Jimmy, today is a painter in Oklahoma. Kevin works for the Pennsylvania Turnpike, and is the greatest hunter I have ever known.

Each brother was a standout in one thing or another. We learned from each other, always sticking together. As my father's business grew we were loved and respected by many in the community.

On weekends I was playing midget football and enjoying fishing and hunting with my brothers.

There was so much love in my home between us all. My dad worked hard at his business and I remember never wanting anything! I had a saint as a mother and a very understanding and loving father.

My mom taught us about an even greater love from a man called God!

My parents and all seven of us Barrows boys…

My mother had her hands full raising all seven of us boys, taking care of our home and making sure we all learned about God. That was very important to her.

So I went to the Corpus Christi Catholic School in Chambersburg, Pennsylvania. There I learned about God, church, basketball and friendship. It was a great school where I had to wear a shirt and tie and became an altar boy, plus my family was very proud of me.

It was at the end of my 9th grade year that my mom and dad sat me down to ask me a very important question.

After attending the catholic school and being an altar boy for nine years, I was given a choice by my parents to stay in my Catholic school and finish out my high school years, or attend the local public school. Seeing all of my neighborhood friends attending public school, I decided to go to the public school in Chambersburg, Pennsylvania where I finished my last three years of high school, and that's where I found all the things that would eventually take my life:

DRINKING, DRUGS, GIRLS. The year was 1981.

This is where I was introduced to all of the things that led to my destruction. Parties, drinking, drugs and women were now my focus on life. I was introduced to all the things that played a role in the end of my life!

Don't get me wrong…It sure was fun, or so I thought. I had a pretty girlfriend, lots of money and the coolest friends in high school.

My friends at school and I tried everything together. I didn't like marijuana because it made me just the opposite of my nickname, "Go-Go"; it made me tired.

When I first started drinking, it was just a thing to do. All my buddies drank; it made me brave and bold. I actually hated the taste but fitting in with my group of friends made me feel important and I wanted to be one of the guys!

When I snuck out to go to bars with my buddies I was always the talkative one, especially when I drank. My mouth got me in more trouble most of the time but, as friends go, we stuck together; all for one and one for all!

The girls came easy. We were all good looking. Back then, alcohol took me places I would have never gone on my own because of my upbringing, but once I started drinking it made me make stupid decisions that would eventually cost me my life.

During those high school years I found girls, girls and more girls. I was a good looking Barrows boy and I had no trouble attracting attention, so I took advantage of that fact.

There were too many girls I went through in my younger years, but there was one special girl that I fell deeply in love with and gave all my attention to…there was just something about her that was different from all the other girls.

She loved me, David! She used a lot of her spare time hanging out with me. We had that special bond.

She was very beautiful and I was proud to walk down the halls of our high school holding her hand.

It was only after she left for college that we drifted apart and I first learned the true meaning of heartache. She broke my heart. I didn't know it at the time, but this was a huge turning point in my life; everything changed. What I didn't know then was that this was the beginning of MY end.

During my high school years my family remained proud of me, never knowing what I was doing behind closed doors. I was sneaking out till all hours of the night, meeting neighborhood friends to drink on the golf course or trying to sneak out with my girlfriend.

I also remember in high school my two best friends, Rob "The Bubbler", and Rob "Sal"; together we were:

'The Three Musketeers'

We spent a lot of our time experimenting with girls, drinking and drugs.

Our summers were spent away from our families in Ocean City, Maryland. I remember thinking we were having the time of our lives. We had more fun than three boys are supposed to have and we never got caught by the law. If we had, we would probably still be in prison for some of the things we did back then.

For me, those summers will be remembered as a mischievous, rich boy who got away with everything. The girls and drugs were abundant, and not being held responsible for anything, I abused it all.

All this partying, drinking, drugging, and chasing women was now my focus on life. It all continued until I graduated from high school. Looking back now, it was nothing short of a miracle we got away with it all…

Today "Rob the Bubbler" is in North Carolina in an oceanfront condo and is enjoying his life fishing and living to the fullest.

Rob "Sal" owns his own printing business in Massachusetts, and is still single.

Rob the Bubbler and David… great day fishing!

One night I was out with a friend and he asked me if I had ever tried coke. Cocaine, I thought, was a horrible 'drug addict' thing only terrible people did. He explained to me that I had the whole cocaine thing wrong. He said it was the most awesome thing to try and that it made you feel great and powerful and not to be afraid to do it. He also told me only the coolest of people did it and it was very expensive and high class too.

That's all it took that day to try my first line of this new drug. He was right! It made me feel awesome! All I wanted from that day forward was *that* feeling and more of it!

If I could see the future and see what this drug was going to do to me I would have never touched, snorted or smoked it. However, I couldn't see the future but I was going to find out the hard way that this drug was MY BIGGEST DEMON!

Front row L to R: My mother, Barbara and my father, Albert
Back row L to R: My brothers; Johnny, Alan, Jeff, Mark, Kevin, David (Me) and Jimmy

CHAPTER THREE:
BEING HELD IN GOD'S HANDS

I was a young boy living with Mom, Dad and all my brothers having the time of my life! My mother had a great friend and neighbor named, Rita Hobbs, who helped my mom with all of us boys and spoke all the time about a man called Jesus.

I really love Rita! She always made me smile and laugh. And, she was married to a man I would later work for and become friends with; Johnny K!

I knew Rita loved The Lord and spoke of Him often. She taught a children's bible study at a local church in Pond Bank, Pennsylvania, and one night she invited me to come along.

Looking back at my life I now understand that it was this woman that led me to my Lord and Savior, Jesus Christ. She showed me in the Bible the verse: John 3:16. That evening I gave my life to God thanks to Rita!

Through the years I've always kept in touch with John and Rita. When I call her up and she answers the phone, I'm always screaming, "RITA, WHAT ARE YOU DOING?"

John and Rita had 2 sons, Michael and David, and a grandson, Logan, who have remained family friends for life.

Now I really understand the saying in the Bible that my God would never leave or forsake me even though I had become a sinner doing things in my life I know displeased Him.

I've also noticed that when someone is in trouble or hurting terribly they always scream out, 'Oh God, Please Help ME'. That's exactly what I said the night before my accident when my God would show me just how unstoppable and powerful He is!

Rita, if you're reading this, I wanted to let you know how very grateful I am you led me to our God!

Rita and Johnny K

CHAPTER FOUR:
HERE COMES "GO-GO"

After graduating high school I had a decision to make; whether to further my education by going to Penn State University or take a place in my father's company.

Well, that decision was an easy one for me. I was sick and tired of school. I had been selling with my dad in his business after school since my 10th grade and I knew what going to work for my dad full-time meant... lots of cash, trips, cruises, plus it meant freedom! I would not have any set hours and I would be the boss over myself and others as well. So, I worked for my dad having to answer to no one.

Working for my dad meant you always had to stay positive! Stay with positive people! Surround yourself with positive thinking and positive actions! That was the one thing that was really important to him and his business.

He said to me one morning when he and I were eating breakfast at Vivian's, his favorite restaurant, "What you breathe in, David, is what you will breathe out!"

At the time I didn't understand that but now I do. It's like if you hang around a dog with fleas, guess what? If you listen to negative words and unhappy people, guess what?

I remember when I started working for dad, our Monday morning sales meetings were all about being positive.

I'm sitting here singing...

'I've got that ole salesman spirit up in my head, down in my feet, deep in my heart. I've got that ole salesman spirit all over me! ... It's all over me to stayyyyy...'

After one of those Monday morning meetings my dad said to me, "David, there are three machines in the trunk of the caddy, two more in the back seat, grab some thousand dollar tickets, we're going to work, son!"

How I miss my dad and his positive outlook on life!

I thought life was good with the latest things in clothes, cars, apartments and especially friends. It was all I knew. For 18 years total I worked as a door-to-door salesman for my dad. Lots and lots of money coupled with a 3-4 day work week made it easy for me to go out drinking, partying and chasing women with the rest of my time.

I always had money and a place I called HOME.

I had gotten so caught up in all this fun I never realized I was actually addicted to alcohol and drugs by this time.

After a few years at my father's business my buddy, Rob, invited me to come live with him.

It didn't take long for "Go-Go" to decide that working for my dad was just work and living in Harrisburg would be fun. So off I went to live with Rob sharing an apartment with him.

There I was introduced to a whole new world of friends, drinking and drugs. This was where I met and married my first wife, Luann. She was just the opposite of me as far as drinking and drugs went, and that is what I liked about her. She also came from money. That meant I was now able to not work, stay home and do nothing but get into trouble.

My wife loved me very much. She bought me a boat, we had a beautiful apartment, but still something was missing in my life.

My friends came to visit, but it was always for the same reason...to use or abuse drinking and drugs.

There is not a drink or a drug that you can tell me about that I haven't done. I experimented with everything, even stuck needles in my arms. I overdosed twice but never enough to scare me into stopping my abuse, unfortunately.

A few years had passed and I found myself hiding so no one would know that I was doing illegal drugs. I spent days, weeks and sometimes months alone in my apartment, hoping no one would miss me. I was down to working only 3 days a week but still making $1,000 a week and no one was questioning me. That soon came to an end. My family found out what I was doing and decided to step in and try to save me from myself.

My family decided it would be a good idea for me to leave Harrisburg to get away from the alcohol and the drugs, so Luann and I moved to Carlisle, Pennsylvania where there was another sales office with a family friend, Leonard. What my family and I didn't realize was I simply couldn't run away from my disease of alcoholism and addiction.

I met a gal named Lynn while I was still married to Luann. Her uncle, Benny, was a mutual friend and employee of my dad's. Benny took me to the Chambersburg Mall one day where she worked.

She was absolutely beautiful and lived in Chambersburg, so it was easy for me to travel back there from time to time to see her.

One thing led to another and I began cheating on my wife with Lynn all while my addictions to alcohol and drugs skyrocketed out of control. Then Lynn became pregnant and when Luann found out we separated and she filed for divorce.

I was full of self-hate not believing what I had done, bottoming out…less than zero if that was even possible. I had boxed myself into a corner with doubts I could ever work my way out.

Yet "Go-Go" still continued to spiral out-of-control…

One of David's best friends "Sal" and David

David's parents: Barbara and Albert Barrows

CHAPTER FIVE:
A STAY WITH FR. MARTIN

I went to my mom and dad's house where I grew up, hoping not to run into any of my brothers. I was going to ask for their help so I could go to my first rehab. I wasn't sure how I would ask but I had no other choices. I figured if I put on my desperate face and cried as though I was at the end of my rope they would feel bad for me and help.

Today I look back to that day in disgrace at how I lied to the only two people who dearly loved me, my parents.

I sat down at my parent's kitchen table, where all the family business was conducted and began crying immediately.

I told them as I sobbed, "I have a problem with drinking and drugs and can't stop, and that's not all...my girlfriend, Lynn's pregnant, Luann knows so it's over between me and her; what am I supposed to do?"

With open arms my mom hugged me and cried real tears telling me God had a plan for me all I needed to do was to walk with Him.

As we sat at that table I was reminded where I came from; a very strong very Christian family; seven boys who stood up for each other; a mother who was a saint and the best of dads. He worked so very hard to give his boys and wife a life that he never had…a house full of love.

I stayed at their house that night. Dad was in disbelief to hear this was happening to one of his sons.

The very next day my dad took me to his favorite place to eat for breakfast; just him and me. We were working together that day and he was teaching me all he knew about his sales business and how to treat others like you want to be treated.

Looking back on it now I think we both had a lot of pent up nervous energy with all that was happening so fast to me.

We ate breakfast at his favorite restaurant where everybody knew him and called him by his nickname, "Kirby".

After coffee and toast we went to his car, a Cadillac of course, which was his favorite possession. Sitting in the parking lot of the restaurant he turned on the car and then he turned to me and said, "I know what's going on and I understand and we are going to get you help".

He then turned the engine to the car off and added, "David, I love you."

Never before had he said that aloud to me! This was the first time in my life my dad let his emotions come out about how he felt about me. That truly was an unforgettable moment he and I shared.

We had made three sales that day, but more importantly, I felt much loved and as close to my dad as ever.

The following day, my dad drove me to my first drug and alcohol rehab, Father Martin's Ashley in Maryland. It is world renowned and one of the top drug and alcohol centers in the country. But it comes with a price; it was very expensive. It also turned out to be the best treatment center I ever would go to.

I was afraid, scared and nervous and my father and I didn't speak very much on the drive there.

I think he knew I was afraid. He again told me he loved me when he dropped me off.

This is where I learned about my addictions. Having the sympathy of my family and friends, I glided through rehab like I was on vacation.

Signing into rehab was long. It took two hours signing all the paperwork. A woman showed me around and took me to my room where I would spend the next 30 days.

Father Martin himself came to my room finding me crying and sitting on the edge of my bed. He sat beside me, put his arm around me and asked if he could say a prayer with me.

From his heart he spoke to God, asking for His protection and care over me. It was from that moment on I not only felt comfortable being there, but just maybe I would learn something about myself I never knew.

Well I did learn something there... I learned I was an addict and alcoholic and if I continued to drink and drug there were only 3 ends to my life; jails, institutions and death.

We had meetings every day, one-on-one counseling, group meetings and graduations of people who were ready to leave after their 30-day stay.

Each week they picked one patient who they thought was the president of that week and he would stand and speak to all the families and friends of those leaving. My goal was to be the president of my class, and I had three weeks to do it.

So, for the next three weeks I became David and not "Go-Go" the addict. I played the game to the best of my ability. I cried when I needed to cry; I smiled when I needed to smile; but, the truth be told, I was not there to learn about addiction. I was there to get back the things I was losing: my family's trust, my job, my wife and my home.

I did it! Graduation came and I was picked to be the most likely to succeed and president of my class. Luann came to my graduation as did my mom and dad.

I spoke with confidence and cried as I talked about what addiction had taken from me. I saw my wife crying in the audience and my heart filled up with love. But little did I know how cunning, baffling and powerful this disease really is.

I graduated with honors, lots of hugs and hope for my future. If I only knew then what I know now maybe I could have stopped addiction from killing me, but my bottom would come years later in an answered prayer I prayed out of desperation one night, but I had many more lessons to learn before that would ever happen...

David speaking at Fr. Martin's at his graduation

CHAPTER SIX:
RELAPSE
(WATCHING THEM FALL)

When I was still married to Luann, returning home from my first drug rehab at Father Martin's it was suggested to go to 90 meetings in 90 days; so I did.

I first noticed how many young people were there. No one could have been over 30 years old, so I fit right in. I was welcomed and made friends quickly. I remember getting my 30 day clean chip one meeting and feeling so proud of myself.

Luann was happy too as I shared my excitement with her. My sponsor at that time, Bob, came to our home and we sat and talked for hours that night.

It gave me a goal. I now had something to look forward to in two months when I would receive my Three Month Clean Chip.

I worked my tail off staying clean and sober for the next nine months of my sobriety. I had gained lots of new friends and a feeling of accomplishment.

One night I had a disagreement with someone at the meeting. I got so angry I decided to walk home and leave my truck in the church parking lot.

Looking back on that evening now I realize I had turned into "Go-Go" and had left David back in the meeting place. As I walked home I was cursing and talking to myself about how I didn't need these people or meetings any longer.

I thought if this is how staying clean was going to make me feel, I might as well start using again.

Well, just that quick is how I first learned about the word RELAPSE.

I had a pocket full of money plus some money I had been hiding for months. I first stopped at a high class restaurant and bar not far from our apartment. I sat by myself at the bar and convinced myself if I would hide it then it was okay for me to just have one. If it wasn't hurting others, and I kept it there at the bar, no one will be the wiser.

Well, for this alcoholic, just one drink was the beginning of a night I can't believe I lived through.

Once I drank one drink the hopelessness consumed me. I sat at that bar for two hours drinking one after another until I was asked to leave. That was fine by me because now I had plans for the 300 dollars I had left.

I met my dealer in a back alley where we use to hook up. He asked me where I had been lately. I lied and said I had been locked up.

I spent the whole night in an abandoned building and hiding from *myself*. I knew what time Luann had to leave for work the next morning, so I walked back home and watched until she left so I could go home and not have to face her. She must have waited up all night for me because she left me a note...

"I hope you're ok. If you need anything, you can call me at work. Love, Luann."

This was the first time I tried to commit suicide...well, not really. I just cut my wrist with a small paring knife, not going deep enough to hit a main artery, just enough to bleed a little and leave me a reminder today of my past.

I've buried too many really great friends, but I never felt as alone as I felt that night when I first relapsed. I not only let Luann down, but I let myself down!

I watch today as others come in and go out of my meetings. I see the same struggles I used to have. I feel so bad when another recovering person falls. But, what I've learned is this:

Recovery is a process. We have to walk before we can run. Time takes time, just keep coming back no matter what! It's okay to make mistakes, just so long as I learn from them. I share my experiences, strength and hope today. It's not about me; it's about WE!

David with one of his signs he lives by today.

CHAPTER SEVEN: GOD SENT STOP SIGNS

When you think of a stop sign you think of driving in your car and having to come to a complete STOP at an intersection.

The reason for these signs is to SAVE LIVES. If there were no stop signs there would be many more accidents at every intersection in this world. People would DIE if it were not for these signs.

Stop signs make us stop what we are doing and then proceed when it is our "turn" to safely do so.

Well, God put many stop signs in my life. It was His way of trying to make me see what I was doing to my life and to the lives of everyone around me, especially the ones that were the dearest to my heart, my family.

However, I wasn't doing so well at reading these signs in my life, quite yet anyway…

Losing Luann was a huge sign I ignored completely and when it was over I moved back in with my parents, just temporarily.

It wasn't long then when I moved in to Lynn's apartment. I was in love with Lynn, a gorgeous woman. At first it was great with all the things young couples do when they are newly in love; and, she was pregnant with my first child!

However, it was so short-lived because I was still using and abusing drugs and alcohol 30 days here and 30 days there; in other words, I was relapsing BAD.

Lynn was a young, pretty girl who wanted to go out and have fun and so did I, so we just fit together well, plus, she was fun to be around.

Looking back to those times, I realize I was about to learn that the power of drugs and alcohol was so great I had thrown away everything and everyone that loved me.

Then, in December, 1992 my son, Bradley, was born. I, of course, was a proud daddy. But, it wasn't long before there was a lot of arguing and fighting with Lynn so I moved back to my parents' house.

Lynn called one day, out of the blue, and calmly asked me to meet her at the Chambersburg Mall. Once there she calmly told me that she met a man and her and Bradley had moved into his apartment.

She just wanted to talk; she wasn't there to argue. Her words still echo in my mind today...

She looked straight at me and said, "You will always be Bradley's dad but I met a man and we are moving to Tennessee."

I hadn't paid Bradley's support regularly and had gone to court a time or two. Once the judge said, "David, I know you and your father, and I know the money you make; so, why are you not paying your child support?"

He continued, "You will end up going to jail if you don't pay it."

Over and over I promised to catch it up, but it never lasted.

So, Lynn presented me with a piece of paper that she held in her hand, along with a pen and said, "David, if you sign this paper all your child support problems will all go away…"

My priorities were all messed up and I signed it not realizing what it meant. I remember thinking at the time, 'She is moving to Tennessee, and you aren't going to see Bradley anyway whether you sign the paper or not…'

So I signed the paper and away went Lynn and Bradley right out of my life.

I threw away my son that day; what was I thinking???? I regretted that day over and over and over again and again…In fact, if I could go back to that point in my life, I would definitely NOT sign that paper. There would be a few other things I wish I could go back and change too, but I hadn't gotten to the point of no return yet!

My son is now a teenager and lives in Tennessee with his mother and new father. Like I said I regret that decision and realize how bad I must have been to even consider it. But it was about to get even worse, much worse...

Even when the money ran out I continued to use by either stealing or selling mine or anyone else's possessions I could get my hands on at the time. My drinking and drugging got markedly worse and there was no stop sign that could stop me.

So once again I moved back in with my parents after Lynn had moved on.

One night after another self-induced party, I went home, very late into the early morning hours, as usual. But this time I noticed something was wrong.

My mom ALWAYS left the porch light on for me but not this night. In fact, all the lights were off in my mom and dad's house including the front porch light!

I thought maybe something happened to my mom because she wouldn't forget about me; she always left the porch light on for me! But this time was different. This time the porch was dark AND the door was locked as well!

I walked around the entire house that night checking all the doors and windows but everything was closed and locked up tighter than I had ever seen.

Later on I would learn my mom and little brother, Jimmy, were inside the house watching me trying to get in. My mom said Jimmy kept wiping the tears from her face as she cried watching her son, David; destroy himself with his obsession.

In desperation that night I crawled in the back of my pickup truck wondering why my family was doing this to poor David....I couldn't see what these drugs and alcohol were doing to me!

I couldn't see what I was doing to all my family; a close family that loved me as much as I loved them. I didn't realize that this was one of God's Stop Signs too!

God tried to put His Stop Signs in my life in the form of rehabs too.

Rehabs forced me to put my life on hold for 30, 60, 90 days, and look and listen to others. But, they couldn't save me from myself and my destructive lifestyle!

It was more like a YIELD sign because I sure didn't STOP.

When my friends died over suicide and overdoses again the Stop Signs were right in front of my face.

I'd never get to say hello to them again. We would never hunt or fish together again. We could never chase girls anymore. If I wanted to see them I'd have to go to a cemetery.

So how cunning, baffling and powerful was my disease? I still wanted to get high and drunk! What was it going to take to stop me?

With my life spiraling downward, the signs weren't working. God had a different plan for me. He would have to come up with a BIGGER SIGN before I would stop.

I had hit rock bottom alright. I was going to die, go into a coma, have brain damage, loose one eye, hurt so bad I'd cry every day, but He would answer my desperate prayer to help me stop…today I celebrate over 10 years clean and sober.

Thank you, God, for that last STOP SIGN! I'm just sorry I couldn't put on the brakes any faster…and, what I had to do to get to that point continued on much longer than I ever thought it would.

David Barrows with the sign God gave him that he uses today.

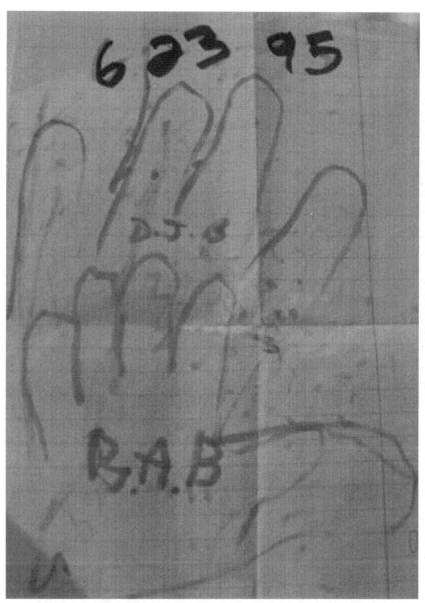

David's and his son, Bradley's hands drawing

The long and winding back roads of my life of alcohol and drugs had more Stop signs and would eventually lead me to my death…

CHAPTER EIGHT:
GOTTA HAVE FAITH

Three rehabs, no job, no money, and living from home to home of friends in Pennsylvania, I was asked to go to work as a salesman for another family friend, Johnny K in Martinsburg, West Virginia.

It was a great move and I'm now working for Johnny K in Martinsburg and still going out and partying every night clubbing, drinking and dancing.

It all began one evening as I was running around single. I didn't have time for a woman. I was in the middle of my addiction and drank every night. I was living in my own apartment I rented across from the office I worked out of. It was close to a lot of drug dealers and in a very bad part of town.

So this one night after work I went out to a local dance club where I could drink and become whoever I wanted, depending on how much I drank. The drunker I got the more lies I would tell perfect strangers.

When I first met Faith, she was with her best friend, Peanut. Faith didn't drink or do drugs, but this was a special night out for her; she was celebrating her divorce and tonight she would drink.

When I first saw her I was taken by her looks; long brown hair, long fingernails and a body to die for. She turned me down the first two times I asked her to dance, but another drink and she agreed.

I don't know what happened out on that dance floor that night, but holding her, smelling her and watching her smile I fell in love.

I can remember trying to impress her with the money I had made that day, buying drink after drink for her, trying to get her drunk and hopefully back to my apartment.

Her friend said they were leaving and going to another bar. I was hurt and figured they didn't like me, but Faith asked me if I would follow them. It didn't take me long to decide I was going, so off to the next dance club I went. For the first time in months I didn't want to do drugs. What I wanted now was something I'd missed for a very long time; a beautiful woman.

At the second bar I had a plan. I would buy shots of Tequila for Faith. Seven shots in all and now when we slow danced I gently kissed her and told her how beautiful I thought she looked.

While at the second bar we danced the night away; laughing, drinking, dancing, all the time thinking I was going to get lucky but that's when I learned a valuable lesson about friendship.

Some time passed and I was then living with two other salesmen that worked with me in Martinsburg, West Virginia for Johnny K. They had rented a mobile home and since I was all but homeless at that time they had invited me to stay with them.

Faith was not interested in sex with me and I didn't understand that. I had never had a woman tell "Go-Go" no! But, that's exactly what she told me! She told me this for six long months of me calling her, taking her on dates and even meeting her family!

For the first time in a long time I had found a true friend who wanted to get to know me for ME!

I was scared of that! What if she found out my drinking and drug using ways...? Would she run away like all the rest, or would she stay with me and watch me kill myself?

We first moved in together at her mom and dad's home in the famous Fox Glen Housing Development in West Virginia.

Her dad was from the old school of fatherhood like my dad was. He took no crap from any man chasing his daughters and was quick to let me know whose house I was living in...HIS!

We made quick friends, Faith's dad and me; he reminded me so much of my father and how family and work were the most important priorities in life! It seemed like all he did was work like my dad did, but when work was over he always had time for his family!

Faith and I soon after moved into our very own first mobile home not far from her mom and dad… but far enough I could hide my drinking and drug using abuse.

We lived not 10 minutes from the town of Martinsburg, West Virginia where it was so very easy to find, get and use all the alcohol I wanted.

It wouldn't be long now until my bottom from alcoholism and drug addiction would cost me my life, but first, enter the angel of my life: Hunter Jacob Barrows.

Hunter was born with a hearing disability, and Faith decided to buy our home and property in Augusta, West Virginia where we had no neighbors, just deer, turkeys (my passion), black bears, and only five miles from the best deaf school in West Virginia; West Virginia School for the Deaf and the Blind located at Romney, West Virginia. So we made the move.

But, no matter where I moved the drug addict and alcoholic continued to follow me. What would it take to get clean?

David and Faith

Grandpa and Grandma Barrows with Hunter

Faith and Hunter

David with his Bible

CHAPTER NINE:
BE CAREFUL
WHAT YOU WISH FOR

For 18 years every night when I went to bed, and because I had learned of God, I prayed and asked him to help me stop. Not thinking that He would ever answer my prayers, my addiction grew worse; I had bottomed out BIG TIME!

Years before, I found hope in a family friend, Rita, who had taken me to a small church in Pond Bank, Pennsylvania and convinced me to turn my life over to God.

I remembered that and asked God to help me.

Be careful what you ask for because He just may answer you like He did me the night of May 27th, 2005.

I never thought God was even listening to me anymore. After all, I turned away from Him years ago after I found alcohol and drugs. They made me feel powerful, never alone, and afraid of nothing!

Well the drinking and the drugs had finally brought me to my knees that night. I was beat and I knew it. All that was left was for me to kill myself to get away from the demon that dwelled inside me. And the name of that demon was:

ADDICITION!

All kinds of thoughts ran through my mind that night; paranoia, fear, isolation, helplessness, hopelessness and total abandonment.

I pray that I NEVER feel that way ever again!

And, as my God was about to answer my desperate prayer, I bent down on my knees, hands folded and raised into the air, I cried out, "Please help me now before I take my own life!"

It was at that very moment I heard footsteps directly above me coming from my son's bedroom.

Was this God speaking to me through my young son or was it my drunken, drugged out mind playing tricks on me again?

I never expected the power of God to enter my mind and body that night, but it happened!

I put down my gun. My body shook as tears rolled down my face. I cried like a baby knowing God's arms were around me, holding me as I surrendered everything to Him.

The phrase from the Bible, "I will never leave or forsake you" was all I could think of.

The following day was the day of my "Miracle" accident. It would be much later, but I was given a gift not many are given, which was a second chance at this thing we call 'Life.'

The next day (the day of my accident) I woke up very early to go turkey hunting on my property. I was alone at first.

There were lots of birds where I lived and turkey hunting was and still is my passion in life.

It was the greatest day I ever had! I felt so much like Hunter's daddy as I woke him shortly after 4:30am to have a quick breakfast, put on all his new camo clothing and asked God to watch over us as we walked to our father/son favorite turkey hunting spot on our property.

With Hunter's hearing loss, I wondered if he would be able to hear the gobbler I roosted the night before.

After the first gobble, he turned to me in our makeshift blind and said, "Dad, did you hear that?"

That answered my question and I smiled as big as he did, if not bigger.

Twenty six gobbles later we were standing over my son's very first Eastern long beard turkey; what a moment we shared that morning together on our mountain.

I harvested a huge turkey. It was 27 pounds and had a 10 inch beard; one of my biggest ever. I was so proud of that bird and the work I put into getting him.

David with his trophy turkey

David and his son, Hunter with their trophies!

We hurried back home to show off the turkey and to get ready to go on vacation. After returning home, I helped to pack our camper for a week-long vacation to Chincoteague Island, Virginia to fish for flounder.

It was one of those days I rarely had, excited, happy and anxious; but that trip would never happen because God had other plans for me.

The camper was packed and Faith and Hunter were ready to go.

Before we left I decided to take a quick ride on my brand new, red, shiny Suzuki Eiger 450 all automatic 4 wheeler before locking it up for the week I'd be gone on vacation. Waving to my family standing in my driveway, I never imagined my life was about to be over.

David on his ATV one last time...

"I'll be right back." I yelled as I backed out the ATV.

I rode to the bottom of my mountain stopping at the neighbors' house where I always went when I wanted to party. Out of that house came a 15 year old boy I knew holding a fifth of vodka, taking a swig of it, he handed it to me saying, "Here you go! Have a drink."

"Hey, Turkey David, can I drive your 4-wheeler?"

"Of course", I said after taking one last swallow of that poison, and away we rode. I got on the back and he climbed in front with his hands on the handle bars and away we went. I was on the back of my new ATV holding on for dear life as he drove off down through the woods.

Looking back now, it was the biggest mistake I ever made.

In less than 30 minutes, I would be dead.

Scene of the accident May 28, 2005

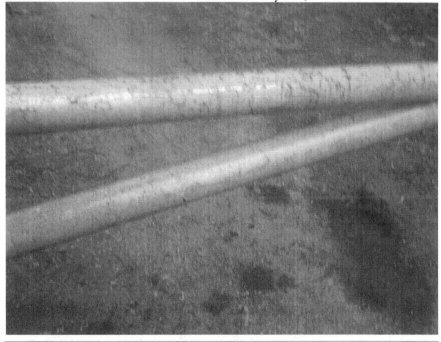

CHAPTER TEN:
THE ACCIDENT

What I am about to tell you now is not from my memory; it comes from the police and EMS emergency reports taken when they found me.

Travelling 50 M.P.H. the young boy ran straight into a back road concrete barrier gate that was designed to stop any vehicles from travelling on this dirt back road. It did its' job too! We stopped.

The driver (the young boy) was thrown over the gate and I met the concrete pole face first.

After getting up and walking back to me, the boy realized I was hurt bad! I wasn't breathing, just bleeding from my entire face and head. He kept yelling at me to get up.

There was a home not 1,000 yards away; a family who I had never met or even knew anything about lived there. He and his wife were inside enjoying the afternoon when he heard a loud crashing sound outside. He went to his front porch and saw the accident.

I was lying beneath the pole motionless and bleeding. My 4-wheeler was still stuck in the pole the boy had run into.

The neighbor rushed back to his wife and told her to call 911… there's been a terrible accident.

Not knowing CPR all he could do was sit beside me, but he knew I was dying. He was a man of God, a minister, so he did the only thing he knew to do…he held me and wiped the blood covering my face. He started praying, asking God to save me.

When I stopped breathing in his arms, he prayed even harder. Knowing I was dying in this man's arms, the driver of the 4-wheeler was yelling my name, pushing on me to get up.

The minister neighbor would later meet me and tell me that he screamed at the teenager to stop pushing me and for him to run to his home and get his wife.

I will never understand why that boy didn't see that bright yellow painted pole road crossing that he had just crashed into.

Why didn't he go around it?

There were 4-wheeler paths on both sides of it.

Did he do this on purpose?

Was he so screwed up on alcohol or drugs that he didn't see it?

As I lay there dying the only thing between life and death was God.

The Slanesville EMS ambulance shows up, sirens blaring and lights flashing and shortly thereafter the Augusta Ambulance Service arrived as well.

I knew the first two paramedics that first reached me. It was a mother and daughter team who worked at the Slanesville EMS Emergency Squad. She couldn't believe her eyes as the mother approached me…covered in blood, my head was cracked wide open. It was the most horrifying thing she had ever seen. Her and her daughter worked on me, trying to find a pulse, bandaging my face and head, cutting off my clothes as they looked for other injuries.

A life-flight helicopter was called but there was nowhere for it to land at my location so arrangements were made to meet it five miles away in a local farmer's field.

My breathing had stopped and there was no movement. The minister was still standing there, praying out loud for God to take me home as the mother of the EMT team gave me a shot of adrenaline and it worked! I coughed and was trying to breathe again.

Covered in my blood, the mother and daughter EMT team loaded me into their ambulance taking me to the helicopter that was waiting to transfer me to Cumberland Emergency Room where doctors awaited my arrival.

I was immediately knocked unconscious as soon as my head hit that pole and oblivious to any of my surroundings and how everyone was desperately working on me to save my life. In fact, the next thing I remember was hearing someone say,

"Welcome back, David, I love you!"

The Slanesville Volunteer Fire Company

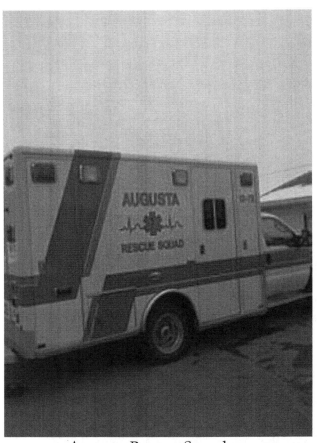

Augusta Rescue Squad

CHAPTER ELEVEN:
MAY 28TH 2005
"GO-GO'S" DEAD

I arrived at the helicopter as fast as the ambulance could drive me there.

Waiting for me were two more EMT nurses and the pilot. They loaded me quickly into the helicopter and took off in the direction of Cumberland Hospital, Maryland.

Working desperately on me, I stopped breathing again. Another shot of adrenaline was administered, but this one didn't work.

The attendants in the helicopter looked at each other and I was pronounced dead on May 28, 2005.

God must have been in that helicopter. He had to of heard my minister neighbor's prayers. God must have known what was deep in my heart to use me as His vessel and speak of His power and glory...when the time was right, but not quite yet.

I coughed and started to choke and breathe again. The paramedics were amazed and again started to work on me.

While I was being transported to the best hospital around that could possibly give me the help I needed to save my life, some woman pulled up in my driveway back home where Faith and the rest of my family were still waiting for me to return (from my "quick" ride on my ATV) so we could take off on vacation.

The kid that was responsible for driving my ATV into the pole had run up to the minister's house and had gotten his wife to take him home. She had the boy give directions to my house at the top of the mountain so she could notify my family.

As she was delivering the news there had been a bad accident and for them to come and follow her and she would take them to the scene; the kid, scared to death, jumps out of the car and runs back down to his house in a flash never showing his face around here again.

The minister's wife takes Faith, Hunter and her parents, Ted and Ruth, to the accident site but the ambulance had already gone. So they went to the Slanesville Fire Hall only to find out I had been flown by helicopter to the Cumberland Maryland hospital.

While Faith, Hunter and Faith's parents were on the hour long drive to the hospital, the helicopter landed at the Cumberland Hospital and the EMTs hurried to get me inside the Critical Care Unit where they were waiting for me to arrive. They had been in constant contact with the helicopter's pilot.

It was like what we see on television but only now it is *real* and it's MY LIFE trying to be saved.

I'm rushed to the Critical Care Unit where I'm met by a room full of people. I'm hooked up to machines. They were putting IVs in both arms. A tube was put down my throat to open up my crushed airway. The bandages were removed and replaced by fresh ones. My blood pressure is going through the roof and I am going into shock. My whole body is shaking as the doctors tried to stabilize me.

My room was full of this hospital's finest doctors, surgeons and nurses; my heart stops beating again and all my vital signs go flat.

After one minute of nothing, I'm pronounced dead AGAIN!

Not giving up on me God enters the room as the surgeon desperately tries to restart my heart for the fifth time! The next attempt didn't work so he asked to recharge it. On the second time he hits me it worked; only by the grace of God and medical technology were they able to resuscitate me.

All my vital signs came back and my heart started to beat again. It was then that I went into a coma.

There were nurses trying to wipe all the blood from my body and removing my bloodstained clothes. Half of my face was gone. From my nose to my ear on the left side there was nothing but broken shattered bone with a part of my brain showing. The head doctor ordered to have me go to the operating room ASAP.

When Faith arrived they wouldn't tell her anything about "John Doe 13" as she was not married to me at the time and they could only release information to his nearest relative. She immediately called my brother, Mark, and he was there in fifteen minutes.

Mark and Faith explained to the hospital personnel that Faith is one paying for the health insurance, and I was on *her* insurance. So they gave her information as long as Mark was there to sign off on everything.

After being wheeled by the nurses on a blood stained stretcher, I was in a hallway on my way to the operating room. Waiting in the hallway hoping to get a look at me were my older brother, Mark, and my Fiancé, Faith Ann. As the nurses stopped briefly, Mark got his first look at me.

"Oh my God, my little brother "Go-Go's" dead!"
He screamed.

The doctor stopped to let Faith know I had a crushed orbital, bleeding from the brain, severe internal injuries, broken bones and he was on his way to reconstruct my face. He told Mark and Faith that the next hour would determine whether I'd live or die.

Faith saw my blood was everywhere on the floor, the walls, and my face was so swollen I was unrecognizable. The only way she could even identify me was when she saw my Black Rose tattoo on my right arm.

The doctor said they needed to call the rest of the family in and they would keep me on life support until they all arrived to say goodbye to me.

Faith said, "NO! He will be fine!"

She didn't believe that anything was going to happen to me and she knew I would be alright even though the doctors kept repeating the severity of my injuries.

My face was a complete mess. I had gone into a coma. The doctors reconstructed my face while the nurses monitored the life support machine that was keeping me alive.

Getting to a telephone, Mark called the entire family telling them to hurry; "Go-Go" is dying, so come say goodbye.

Faith was on the phone with my brother, Alan's wife, Robin who was in the medical field and was explaining the severity of my injuries. Again Faith did not believe anything bad was going to happen to me. She insisted I would be fine.

The doctors kept coming out and saying it would be a miracle if I made it within the next hour, then it was within the next four hours and then it was within the next eight hours and then it was within the next twelve hours...

All Mark could think about was the fun times we had together hunting, salmon fishing, selling, chasing women and, of course, our not so well kept secret of getting high together, using cocaine, smoking crack, and eventually finding crystal meth.

He needed a moment to be alone with his thoughts so he went outside to smoke a cigarette and he made a deal with God, saying, "Please God, save my little brother, David. If you will do that I promise not to use drugs anymore."

Not knowing if God heard him, he drops to his knees in the middle of a crowded area where people could see him. Tears filled up his eyes thinking "Go-Go" was dead and he could never see him alive again.

Well, God was listening to Mark that day and heard his desperate prayers.

Mark now is clean from drugs and comes to meetings with me when he can find time from his busy life. He calls me every day making me laugh and we now have an unbreakable brotherly bond. We have fished together and chased Longbeard turkeys since my accident. But what I cherish the most is I have my big brother, Mark, back clean and sober.

Thank you, Lord!

But, I wasn't 'out of the woods' yet and still had a long way to go...

David's brother, Mark, and David

CHAPTER TWELVE:
OPEN YOUR EYES NOW!

The memory from my accident in May, 2005 will live in my heart forever. I was never a big religious person. I believed in God and from time to time went to church. But God was not the first thing on my mind every day.

What happened to me the day of my ATV accident will forever be the most important day of my life.

My father passed away in 2004 which was a year before my accident. I actually got to see him one more time after my accident while I was in my coma.

Somewhere between the ground I laid dying on and coming out of my coma, I witnessed my deceased father reaching for my hand and walking with me until we stopped to talk.

My dad never looked so peaceful or so happy. He told me he loved me and said God did too. He asked me to go back home and raise my own son as he had raised me.

As my dad let go of my hand and slowly walked away I noticed my surroundings. It was the most beautiful place I've ever seen. I was at peace and didn't want to leave.

Hearing my dad's instructions, I heard a voice telling me to 'open my eyes'. The voice was coming from my mother.

She said, "Welcome back, David, I love you!"

Everyone was happy to finally have me out of my coma, and when I did wake up I began the fight of my life.

But what I didn't know was my body had already been through so many fights I have no memory of, including detox. I was filled in on what all had happened while I had been in my coma. I learned that Faith and Hunter had stayed by my side as much as they could. Mom and the boys came often too. As always, my family rallied by my side.

Brothers Jeff, Jimmy and my mom came the next day after my accident. Jimmy stayed for a couple of days for Faith because by Sunday afternoon Faith had been up since Saturday morning and finally lost it Sunday evening. She finally broke down and all the emotions came out: ANGER FEAR AND THE REALITY OF IT ALL HIT, and hit her hard.

When Jimmy saw how Faith was emotionally, he took it upon himself to see to it she got some sleep. She had been awake so long and everything was finally soaking in and she was starting to unravel. The hospital gave her a room to sleep in and he stayed there with her to make sure no one bothered her so she could get her rest.

I had lots of visitors while I was hospitalized besides my immediate family.

I am so fortunate to actually have a second family, The Eby Family from Beans Cove, Pennsylvania who own a lumber mill where my brother, Mark worked.

From time to time I would stay at Mark's where I would work alongside him all night long!

There were four of the Eby boys: Conrad, Durrell, Llewelyn and Truman. They came often to my hospital bed and prayed over me and gave constant support to my family.

Finally the day they had all been waiting on arrived. I opened my eyes. I was finally awake from my long coma.

When I first woke up I didn't know who I was or where I was. I just knew I was surrounded by doctors and nurses, machines and tubes coming out of my mouth, going down my throat, under my belly button going into my stomach and another one underneath my right arm, a life support machine and IVs in both arms.

I could only see from one eye and one side of my face had no feeling and was bandaged... my mom was right there holding my hand when I woke up and I didn't even know her. I could feel her gripping my hand tight.

That is when I was to hear my fate. They explained my face had been reconstructed. I wasn't expected to ever be able to walk or talk again. I had to learn how to use my 'new' body and mind.

As I woke up I was told I couldn't move too much because there was still bleeding. I had no idea what had happened and what was going on at all!

I eventually pulled out my feeding tube and almost had the chest tube pulled out. The nurses had to put mitten-like things on my hands to keep me from pulling out all my tubes and IVs which were in each arm.

So, like I said, my family rallied by my side during those long days and helped each other as well as be there for me when I would wake up.

All of my vitals were stable but they tried to limit visiting time in the room with me after I woke up to just one person and only five minutes at a time so I would remain calm.

Faith knew I was going to be alright she just didn't know how I would be. She thought me being paralyzed was a big possibility and talking skills were nothing at first except grunts. I had to learn how to walk and talk again. But first, I had to learn who I was and who EVERYONE ELSE was!

I didn't recognize anyone! My mom brought me her family picture albums and showed me all my family and the homes we had lived in. She talked about my dad and his business and how I had sold for his business for 18 years.

Mark, Jimmy, Mom and Faith were with me the entire time during my accident recovery.

Slowly my family and friends would talk to me and my long term memory FINALLY came back!

Soon after I woke up I heard another familiar voice. It was my first sponsor, Bob.

"David, I love you and have you had enough yet?" he said as his body leaned over mine.

This certainly was not the first time I had heard that said to me by this guy.

When I went to my first rehab it was recommended I do 90 meetings in 90 days and I was doing my 90 meetings in 90 days when I met Bob. When he spoke it was exactly like my story. He really spoke to my heart. I knew exactly what he was all about. At the end of that meeting I had sought him out to talk.

Bob became my first sponsor. And then one year later I relapsed which ended me in prison for several months. When they released me, there in the parking lot was Bob, my sponsor, waiting to pick me up.

"David I love you! Have you had enough yet?" he said to me.

I said, "Yes, I'm in the parking lot of the prison I was just released from, yes, I've had ENOUGH, Bob!"

Well I guess I was wrong. There were plenty more bad things that had happened since then but, yes, NOW I FINALLY KNEW after this accident that there truly really are only three outcomes to alcoholism and drug addiction:

JAILS – INSTITUTIONS – DEATH...

And, YES, Bob, I HAVE *FINALLY* HAD ENOUGH!

But, there were lots more hurdles to jump down the road to healing from my accident…

David after his accident, 2005

David and his mother, Barbara

L to R front row: Mark, Mom, Kevin
L to R back row: Jimmy, Alan, Jeff and David

Front row: David and his son, Hunter, right behind him
Back row: Johnny, Kevin, Mark, Barbara and Alan

Barbie and Johnny Barrows

David and Barbara 2015

CHAPTER THIRTEEN:
MY HEROES;
MICAH AND TRACY

I showed everyone at that hospital it wasn't quite over for me even though I still can't feel my left arm, left leg, or face yet today. And, it didn't come easy either.

I spent months there before I was transported to the world's greatest rehab hospital in West Virginia: Health South Rehab in Morgantown, West Virginia. There I was introduced to a team of physical therapists who would become my saviors of my own self.

I hated me and what I had become: a brain damaged, coma-boy, alcoholic, drug addicted, ATV accident victim.

Lucky for me there were some people that didn't see me in the same light.

Tracy Rice and Micah Anthony, who were to be my therapists, were assigned to make me walk and talk again, but I sure didn't make it easy on them or me…

I was about to meet my physical therapist team at the Health South Hospital, but little did I know I was also about to meet the two most amazing women I ever would come to know.

They had just finished working with and helping the boy from West Virginia who was the sole survivor of a coal mining accident that shocked the entire world.

How was I to compete for their attention only being an ATV accident survivor who had just awoke from a coma?

Well I found out fast that it wasn't their job; it was their life! They were the most loving, caring, toughest therapists EVER.

For example, her shift was over and it was time for Micah to go home to her husband and child. As she walked by my room she stopped to say 'see 'ya in the morning, Dave' when she found me crying in my special netted-bed, which my family and I had nicknamed my Spiderman bed.

She pulled up a chair and for the next hour she sat with me listening and talking. I don't know if she even remembers this, but she stopped my confusion and hurt and showed me a small piece of her heart that day.

Was that her job? No, that was Micah Anthony, the most beautiful woman in the world to me at that moment with a heart of pure gold!

Micah also is the one who I've told so many people how she got me out of my wheelchair one day in therapy class. Micah, if you're reading this, thank you so much for being you and MAKING me walk again…

Now to Tracy Rice, the therapist we all wanted, sometimes I think I should get into another accident so SHE could help me again!

She was beautiful, a picture perfect woman. She had everything most women only dream of; a perfect life, body, husband and kids. But, I found out quickly she meant business at her work and life.

She took me down to a room where there was a small set of steps for me to climb. It was only three steps up and three steps down; I could do it!

My brain at first didn't know how to walk stairs.

Putting her arm around me and holding my other arm, Tracy said this to me,

"Together we will learn to do this, David. Just walk with me. I'm right beside you."

So, as each day passed I got better. I went further and it wasn't long until I was climbing all the steps, all six of them, three up and down!

She sat with me at lunch a few times, eating and laughing, taking my mind off the loss of my left eye and my daily pain.

When Faith wasn't there, I flirted with these two women only to be reminded by them they were married.

Micah a few years back at one of Tracy's talk she said to me, "David, tell everyone the Bee in the Pants story."
This is what happened. One day in therapy class I told Micah I had a bee in my pants and it was stinging me and could she please help me.
Micah said, "YOU don't have a Bee in Your Pants!"

Another thing Micah did was she got me out of my wheelchair and got me to take my first step. One day Micah turned on and off the lights to get our attention. Every one stopped what they were doing. She walked directly over to me, David.

Micah puts her hands on her hips and says, "Today is the day, David; today you walk!"

Angrily I reply some words I should never have said. I said, "Look, Bitch, I guess you don't know what the doctors have told me that I will never walk again!"

Micah returned fire with, "I don't care what the doctors have said or what the papers say. TODAY is the DAY YOU WALK!"

She continues to stand there a long five minutes with her hands on her hips, standing there in silence. I have the entire room of 15-20 patients all with their eyes on me.

Everyone was looking at David. I am so angry she pointed me out and made a spectacle out of me. I am silent, and then I start to cry.

She knew (because she is a great therapist) the longer she stood there David would react.

I start to feel sorry for myself. I am never going to walk again. My face is half gone, I am miserable and all these emotions begin to pour out with my tears.

Micah is still standing over me and she leans down and she said, "WE can do this. Just stand from your wheelchair. I am here to help you."

She has walked this road with me so far and I am literally crying my eyes out. I, out of anger, say, "Okay, Bitch, I will show you, but when I fall, you will have to pick me up!"

She stands back with hands on hips again, waiting for me to stand up.

I was so angry I was determined to prove her wrong, so I say, "…okay I'm gonna do this…"

I took my left hand and put it on the arm of the wheelchair. I take my right hand and put it on the other arm of the wheelchair and with all the strength I could muster, I begin to force myself up with the strength of my arms, (because my legs were like rubber bands) and I force myself right out of the wheelchair.

Micah is still just standing there. Little by little she is encouraging me to lift off of the seat and I am looking at her as she is nodding her head to continue.

My knees start to bend. I'm holding on with all my might onto this wheel chair and I try to get as straight as I could. I close my eyes, grit my teeth, and with all the might I have left, I push as hard as I could to raise my body.

I feel my legs starting to shake out of weakness, uncontrollably, so I lock my knees and still holding on to the wheelchair tears begin falling from my face. I'm angry.

The next thing I feel is Micah's hand on my shoulder and I open my eyes and I am standing face to face with Micah and she says, "Now, look down!"

And, at that very moment I can't believe it! I'm standing up! ...and they told me I would never walk again.

Micah said with a huge smile, "David, WE *will walk again!*"

From that day forward not only was she my hero, I knew that if I believed in those two women I could do anything.

It wasn't long after that I couldn't wait to get to therapy instead of feeling dread like before.

Before I knew it, WE were walking EVERYWHERE!

POWERFUL, POWERFUL STUFF MIRACLE WORKER!

Looking back now, I was blessed to have these two women as my friends and therapists. I still have daily contact with both of them as they are both my friends on Facebook.

By the way, ladies, I will never be able to thank you enough for helping and putting up with me…

There actually are NO WORDS to explain what Tracy Rice has given me but I will try. She gave me back ME, but not that broken me, a new, BETTER THAN EVER ME!

She continues to encourage me to this very day. I go yearly and give talks at her university. It gives me great pleasure to give her all the glory, but she reminds me, time and again, it isn't about ME … it's about WE!

Still, there was so much more for me to learn…this was just the beginning!

Tracy Rice and David

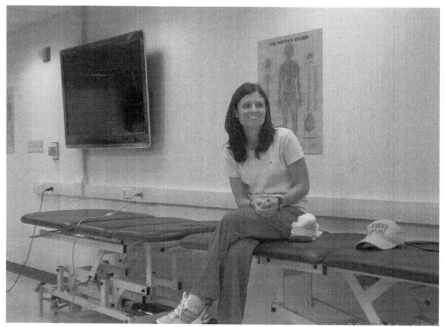

Micah

CHAPTER FOURTEEN:
HOME

I remember the big day at Health South Rehab Hospital in Morgantown when I was to meet with all my doctors, therapists, counselors, and my family.

It was going to be determined whether I was physically and mentally able to return home after my long stay there healing from my miracle accident.

After the meeting had started, it looked as though I was going to get approval to leave. Micah, my therapist, spoke up and stated she didn't feel it was in my best interest to return home yet due to my physical and mental limitations.

My heart dropped to the floor as she spoke but I knew she only wanted what was best for me.

My brain damaged mind for the first time was thinking, 'What could I think to say to allow these people to let me go home?' I said the first thing that came to my broken mind.

"Excuse me," I heard myself saying. "My personal nurse, Mariam Graham, will be moving into my house to care for me as she is an R.N. and great family friend."

She did care for older ladies at her Mennonite home, however, was never asked or considered to care for me. She had her hands full with her ladies and husband; the famous Dale Graham from Beans Cove, Pennsylvania.

Of course, after I spoke, Faith straightened out my lie and left the decision to my doctors and their therapists.

I was crying but surrounded by the people who loved me the most and only wanted what was best for me

I closed my eyes and spoke once again a silent prayer asking God for His Will in another important decision that was being made once again with my life.

The doctor then said, "David, you have been through a terrible storm," as he went through my list of physical and mental disabilities now. He finished by saving, "I know you want to go home so the decision is up to you, Son... do you want to go home today?"

Of course my answer was, "YES!"

What I was about to learn next was the power, strength and wisdom of yet another woman who I had known for some years. Her name was Ruth Kranenberg and she was Faith's mother and Hunter's grandmother. She would interrupt her entire life and move into my home along with her husband, Ted, for an entire year!

She drove me to all my outpatient therapy sessions at first. But, not long after the classes would take place at my home since I was afraid to get out into the public.

She drove Hunter back and forth to school, she cooked, she cleaned, and she even walked with me on my daily exercise therapy walks outside on our mountain.

She was an extremely strong woman mentally and physically. She put her foot down when my mouth got me into trouble, which seemed like a daily event.

This woman was not only an answer to my prayers, but a huge stepping stone in my recovery.

Thank you, Ruth, once again for helping to save me from myself!

Ruth Kranenberg and David

CHAPTER FIFTEEN: MY NEW BEGINNING

With my rehabilitation finally finished, I was released to go home. Faith and Hunter were there to pick me up.

The ride home was horrible. Every little bump set me off but I got through it. It would take a long time for me to be able to relax going down a road riding in anything! The accident had traumatized me in the worst way.

As soon as I got home the only thing I could think of was the accident site. I wanted to see where it all happened. I *needed* to see it since I had no real knowledge of it; I wanted to understand how it all happened.

I also wanted to see where this man, my minister neighbor, lived. I wanted to see the pole that did all this damage to my body and my mind.

"Are you SURE you want to see it, David?" Faith asked, unsure herself if it was a good idea for any of them to go back to that horrible spot.

"YES!" was my most definitive answer.

So Faith and Hunter took me to the accident site along with her father and mother.

As we pulled up to the spot my emotions were everywhere. The dirty, back country road was bumpy leading right up to the pole that stole my life.

I remember that day like it was yesterday. It was a very hot, muggy day out and very dusty and dirty.

Faith's dad led me up to the yellow metal pole gate that still guarded the area.

Part of the pole was bent...Knowing what that bend was caused from; I grabbed onto it with both hands and thought *'this is where IT happened'!*

Crying now and visibly shaken, Ted came up to me and tried to comfort me.

"My life is never going to be the same!" I cried out in pain.

"No, it's not...it's gonna be better!" Ted reassured me.

All I could think of was the opposite of what he was saying. How could my life get better? I can no longer feel the left side of my body, I drool like an old person, when I look in the mirror the face I see isn't ME! All I could do is to think how miserable the rest of my life was going to be.

I slumped down and sat with the pole up against my back. Sweat ran down my entire body with the heat, or maybe it was just from my anger and frustration. I started shaking and anger overtook me just thinking about the boy who did this to me!

He never got as much as a scrape. Yet I ended up like this…

Sadness took over my anger and I put my face in both hands and sobbed.

After a few minutes Faith and Ted came over to me and led me back to the car. The ride back home was quiet but the thoughts in my mind were going everywhere. All I could think about were the three letters that the doctors at Health South had told me that I would have to deal with which was T.B.I. Traumatic Brain Injury!

I would never be the same again. All I could think of at that moment was that I would be better off dead than alive if I had to live like this, damaged pieces of my former self.

I didn't want Hunter to see me like this so I went back down to the basement where I could grieve in solitude.

What will I do with my life now? My body was so battered and bruised, brain damaged, drug and alcohol addicted, sight lost in one eye and feeling worthless; I was devastated.

This was something new I was gonna have to figure out how to deal with…

I should never have left Health South…I was safe there. Now I am back out in the cold, cruel world and there was no one to hold my hand and encourage me like Tracy and Micah did.

I needed to talk to Tracy. I knew she would help me feel better. She was the only one that could help me now. I leaned on her plenty after I got home and still do today. She became my hero. If it wasn't for her and so many others I don't think I could have made it through the roughest parts of starting over.

I learned that everyone is in your life for a reason, some come in for a day or even just a moment in your line at the grocery store, others remain a vital part of your life forever. I was soon going to see some of each...and how God was going to put me in others' lives as well. I was about to become:

"The West Virginia Miracle Man"!

Tracy Rice and David

CHAPTER SIXTEEN:
JESUS LOVES YOU!
(Alligator Angie)

Months of therapy at the hospital and lots of tears later, when I returned home to West Virginia, I was told I'd never work again.

My first thoughts were of happiness of never having to work again. But, just my daily exercise program with my home therapist, I was afraid. In fact, I was afraid of everything!

The thought of leaving my home paralyzed me. I was scared to death of the outside world. I was afraid of the wind, the trees, and mostly people. I couldn't handle any type of crowd anywhere. While I still needed physical therapy at home, I could not get myself out the door because of my fears, so the therapists came to me. I was completely isolated at this point and cut off from the world. I couldn't even go to the grocery store! I cried all the time.

One of my therapists suggested that I could start getting back into the world by going on the internet, so I started playing on my old computer. I got a My Space account and then a Facebook one later on. It kept me busy and my mind off of my intense pain each day.

Before long I moved over to Facebook exclusively. I lived my life through Facebook then and still enjoy it even now.

That is how I found Alligator Angie. I noticed on Facebook a woman named Angie, who was married, had children and was a bible reading Christian.

The thought of this woman and how she walked this walk with me from the very start of my new life still makes me cry today. I have never even met this woman, but what she has done for me was definitely an answered prayer.

I'm told God puts people in our lives for a reason and I will never be able to thank and praise God enough for bringing me Angie. I learned the value of a true friend through her, and, because of her help and inspiration, I'm closer to my God today.

For the first time since my return home from my accident, I trusted a complete stranger with my whole life. I couldn't wait to tell her of my experience with seeing my deceased dad, holding his hand and speaking to him.

The brain damage from the accident made me scared and afraid all the time, but one day Angie told me that I was NEVER alone; God was with me all the time. That's all it took!

I still had daily work I had to do to heal my broken body; lots of exercises to strengthen my muscles, lots of brain memorizing work, but now, I was able to go outside and take short walks ALL ALONE.

Angie and I continued to talk to each other and even did a bible study together, on line of course.

Every day and every step, from that day forward God and I walked together. I remember telling Angie if anyone had seen me walking, they would think I was weird because I spoke out loud to God while He and I walked.

Angie would listen to me complain about my reconstructed face and the pain I dealt with every day. She would then email me a video of a man with no arms and no legs who was reaching out to others who had hurt him…and he was happy, so what did I have to complain about?

She prayed with me over the phone, I prayed as well, thinking, 'I hope I do this right', but she explained to me that there is no wrong way to talk to God.

Today I praise and glorify God all the time. I read my Bible, and as each new day arrives I grow closer to Him and my new best friend, Alligator Angie. By the way Angie…Jesus loves you!

Alligator Angie

CHAPTER SEVENTEEN:
A GIFT FROM GOD
(MY SPONSOR)

I had been home for three months now and my physical therapy was almost finished here at home. I remembered Tracy and Micah saying that my first year being home was the biggest year for my healing. So I pushed and pushed and pushed that first year.

I still had a lot of mental illness but my body was as good as it was going to get. I continued my exercises, but now, I did it without a therapist coming to my home daily.

For the first year, Faith's mother moved in with us to help with Hunter and any driving wherever I needed to go like hospitals, doctors, grocery stores, etc…something was definitely different about me now. Yes, I hurt terribly and was seeing my family doctor every week, but I hadn't taken a drink or drug for over a year. That by itself astonished me.

Before my accident, I couldn't go one day without a drink or drug. But now, the obsession was gone! Where did it go? Why do I not want anything to make me feel better, or worse?

After talking to my doctor and some family members, it was suggested I go to drug and alcohol meetings again and just listen this time. So, that's what I did. I went to my first meeting and picked up my one year clean and sober medallion.

It was an overwhelming accomplishment that I didn't think I earned. I was in a coma, at hospitals, rehab facilities and more doctors' offices than I could count. I wasn't free to choose to drink or drug, but God knew exactly what He was doing with this drug addicted alcoholic. He was giving me a memory to carry for the rest of my life what alcohol and drugs did to me.

So, I picked up a meeting list, and from that day forward I started to go every night. I knew I needed a sponsor at these meetings. A sponsor is someone I had something in common with and someone I trusted with my life. Meeting after meeting I would go, listening to others and learning a new way of life.

One evening I went to a local church where there was an eight o'clock meeting. I showed up at 7:45pm to talk and meet others. I was told that night there was a speaker sharing his story, so I was excited to just listen.

His name was Rich A. and he had 40 years of sobriety. Listening to his story was like listening to my own story.

The things he had done, the things he had lost, the life he had ruined for another drink was *my story*! How did he hear my story? Did someone tell him how I sold all my possessions for one more hit of crack, coke or drink?

No, it was *his story too*; he lived to tell his amazing testimony of his life being interrupted by God and given a second chance to live through this program of AA.

He spoke to my heart that evening. I cried as I listened to him sharing to a roomful of drunks and addicts how his life today is not run by him. He has turned his will over to God and has 40 years of sobriety to prove it.

He tells me every day, we live only for Today. Yesterday is gone, Tomorrow may never come; all we have is this wonderful gift from God called Today! So, yes, I asked Rich to be my sponsor that night. We became great friends.

He helps me walk this walk of sobriety. It hasn't been easy. I've had a lot of mountains to climb in recovery, but, with God on one side of me and Rich on the other, I have a great chance of staying clean and sober just for Today...By the way, Rich, if you ever read this, I wanna say Thank You from the bottom of my heart. You took a broken man and helped put me back together.

Cindy S., Carol, George, John, Dave and Mike are all valuable helpers at my home group for my AA meetings. They are STONE COLD AA and that is what I need so I will not drink today. AA people are such great help to me!

I have help wherever I am and it is very comforting to know someone's always got my back…and now YOU KNOW someone can have your back too, or the back of a loved one that is hurting from drugs or alcohol like me. All that is required is to make that first step forward to getting the help. The group will be here waiting for you with open arms!

Tearcoat Church, Augusta, West Virginia

This church is where my home group meets every Tuesday night in Augusta, West Virginia at 8pm. It is at this group where I celebrate my year of clean and sober every year. Stop by ANYTIME

CHAPTER EIGHTEEN:
DAD'S GIFT

After my accident I had been home for a while and doing my therapy when my little brother, Jimmy, and his fiancé, Sammy, came to visit me. I told him I had something that I needed to tell my mom, something important that had to be face-to-face and not over the telephone.

I was still very new to the outside world just recently being released from the hospital and very scared of everything, but in my heart, I knew I had to sit with her and explain in detail what had happened to me in that hospital.

Jimmy and Sammy said they'd take me to Mom's and so we all started the two hour drive to Penn National Estates, Fayetteville Pennsylvania.

My mother had been a saint through the entire episode of my accident.

She was so glad to see me the first time outside of that hospital. She was giving me kisses and welcoming me back home.

The conversation started like every other conversation I had with my mom. She reached for me and hugged me like there was no tomorrow! I could see she was still the strong woman that raised seven boys but could also see she had questions for me about why I was there.

"MOM", I said. "I need to tell you something that I haven't told you and I want your full 'Mother's attention'."

She stopped what she was doing.

"David, fine, whatever you want. Let's go out into your father's garage."

The garage had been Dad's favorite place to be when he wasn't doing his vacuum sales business, so this was the perfect spot!

My mom took chairs and put them in a little circle for the four of us.

She asked me if I wanted something to eat or drink but I was too excited for that; I just wanted to jump right in with my excitement to tell her what I had experienced!

After all the welcomes, hugs and kisses, we sat across from one another. She held tightly to her photo album she had brought out to show me pictures of our past growing up. The pictures were of all her boys, of course, and her and dad.

Dad's passions had been for his sons, teaching them to work hard...playing hard with his boats, fishing trips, and his favorite thing to do... cleaning his yard! Mowing the grass, picking up the leaves and just riding his riding lawnmower seemed to give him peace and pride like nothing else.

I didn't want to get into all of that with my mom that day because I had exciting news about my dad, her husband, who had gone to heaven not long before my accident! So I got right into it with her!

I said, "Mom I have to tell you something about Dad and I'm not sure how to tell you so I will just tell you."

As she put the photo album beside her chair, she just smiled at me and said, "Okay David, tell me about you and your dad."

I immediately started to cry.

"What's wrong, David? Are you hurt?" she asked.
Mom tried to comfort me.

"I'm afraid to tell you what I have to tell you." I said.

"David, I love you and don't ever be afraid to tell me anything," she assured me. "There's nothing that you could ever do that would make you lose your mother's love, so tell me, please!"

"Okay, Mom, here is what happened." I started crying hard.

She said, "Are you hurt?"

"No, I don't know how to tell you this is all," I answered.

"What?"

I gathered myself. My little brother leaned over and punched me in my good arm and said, "What's up, Go, you okay?"

"I'm fine, Jimmy. Okay, here is what happened…I saw Dad!" I cried out. I cried as I continued to speak.

"Somewhere between hitting the pole and coming out of my coma I found myself in an unfamiliar place. I was lying on a bed hearing my name being called…"David, David, David…"

"As I turned my head, I saw my father standing over me reaching his hand out to me. I reached up and his hand met in mine and I felt it. I heard my name being called, 'David, David, David' over and over. I turn my head to the right and I find myself a in a bed. There are white sheets and a pillow under my head and I'm lying down. The room was empty and the walls were white, like cloud white. I open my eyes and I don't know how to tell you this Mom…"

Jimmy put his arm on my shoulder to give me strength, so I continued.

"There was someone standing over top of me reaching out as if to take my hand, so I put my right hand out and reached for him…it's MY DAD!"

"When my hand hit his hand I could feel it… it was such a real feeling. I knew at that moment IT WAS REAL! If I hadn't felt his hand in mine I don't think it would have been as real to me. But it really was MY DAD pulling on my hand. I'm with my dad again…Oh my GOD!"

"I take my feet and swing out of my bed and I stand up face-to-face with my dad, who had been dead for over a year."

"Soon after that, he began to talk and I began to walk with him."

"I'm walking with my dad and I can't believe it. Is this real or a dream? I start to see and realize my surroundings a bit. I am in the most beautiful place ever."

"At this place, the colors surrounding me are almost iridescent. The prettiest blue ever… all the colors are so bright and prettier than I could have imagined."

"I'm walking in a fog around my feet; a misty fog. I don't hear anything or see anyone else but this fog and my dad and all the beautiful colors. The fog moves with our steps."

"I feel loved, cared for and more than welcome. I don't know where I am but I am supposed to be there. I can just feel it is the place I need to be."

"THERE WAS NO PAIN, NO HURT, NO ANGER, NOTHING BUT GOOD WELCOMING FEELINGS, CARING AND MY DAD."

"I WAS SPENDING A MOMENT IN HEAVEN! I WAS ABOUT TO MEET GOD AND I KNEW IT."

"Surrounded by the beauty, we didn't walk far and Dad stops walking abruptly. He squeezes and holds tighter to my hand, then he suddenly stopped and faced me. He looked younger than the last time I had seen him, lying in his bed, at his home, with the Hospice people there helping us deal with his passing away. He looked young, happy and very handsome. As we stood there facing each other, he spoke to me saying, 'David, I love you.' 'I love you too, Dad' I told him. He then said, 'God loves you, too'."

"I told him I knew God loved me. He then said these words to me which I will hold forever in my heart…"

"'It's not time for you to be here yet, David. I want you to go back home and raise your son as I raised you!' "

"As soon as he said that, he let go of my hand and I found myself back in the bed. I felt like my new life had just been born. My life was starting over with another gift from God."

The doctors now say that's when I came out of my coma. There are no medical reasons why I did survive, why I'm walking, talking, driving, fishing, hunting and raising my son today. The only true reason is that God had plans for me and He gave me a second chance at this thing we call life.

It took me an hour crying with my brother's hand on my shoulder to get through it all. I finally had my mom's full and undivided attention.

When I was finished telling them the story, I told them I had told no one else except the doctors.

Sammy, Jimmy, my mom and I all four were sitting there crying.

Mom was overwhelmed because she missed her husband, so she started asking me questions.

"David, you have been touched by the hand of God!" she said, and then she added, "What did Al look like?"

"He didn't look like when I last saw him on his death bed with hospice saying goodbye." I continued. "He looked terrible back then, but when I saw my dad in heaven he was more than beautiful. He looked great, Mom, handsome, young, smiling and happy. I didn't want to leave him or Heaven."

"I want to see some old pics of Dad." I said suddenly.

Mom quickly got back out her album and showed me some pictures of Dad.

I looked through the pictures until I found the one that I recognized.

"THAT'S what he looked like when I saw him; tall, handsome, hair done, a good looking man."

Mom looked up from the picture I was pointing to and said, "David that is when your dad was 35 years old. It was his service picture and he *was* young and handsome and strong."

"Mom, he's ok…he's fine. And, Heaven is all the things you and he taught us boys it was… how we never really die if we believe in Jesus Christ. It's all true, Mom. I know I told you some things in the hospital, but Dad was with me the entire time…he came to me sometime in my coma!!!"

"He was holding out his hand to me like this mom…." I said holding out my hand towards my mom…

"Dad talked to me, Mom. He told me it wasn't my time to be there yet. He said for me to go back home and raise Hunter as he raised me." I continued.

The more I talked to my mom the more excited I got. She could tell what she was hearing was how her God had answered her prayers and came to me during this accident.

Her God had sent my dad to stand with me in the most beautiful place I had ever witnessed. It was Heaven and I knew it. I got to witness first-hand what was waiting for me after my body dies and my life ends on this earth!

I was going to be with my dad again, and he was showing the place to me, and it was Paradise…the three of them sat there in Dad's garage that afternoon just listening to my excitement. I explained about finally finding the truth about what she and dad had always taught us growing up.

I told her Dad was waiting for us, he was more than great, he was happy! He was handsome; he was in a place that is so beautiful, no hurt, no pain, no problems, just beauty, peace, love and joy.

After I finished my mom cried, uncontrollably at first, then she stood up and held her arms out to me wanting a hug. She hugged me tighter that day than ever before. She hugged me like only my mom hugged, and said,

"I've been teaching you boys about the power of our God and how real He truly is! Now you know how UNSTOPPABLE He really is. Your dad and I have tried all our lives to point you to Him."

"David, I'm so happy you have returned home. This is where our God needs you to be. Now, do as you father told you and raise your son, Hunter, like he raised you!"

David and his mother, Barbara

I told this story later in my church and cried as I described my surroundings at that precious moment. It was unlike anything I'd ever seen. I'd been all around the world with my dad's business, seeing places like the Bahamas, Florida, The Great Lakes and Niagara Falls, but nothing compared to this place.

This place was absolutely beautiful. Not only did it look beautiful, but it smelled and felt like home. It was welcoming. I didn't understand it at the time, but later I would be told I had actually spent a moment in Heaven, walking with my dad.

Today I am NOT just a believer in God and Heaven, but I am one of God's Soldiers. Any chance I get, I speak of my story, all over the country or where I live, every night of the week I speak at local meetings, churches, organizations.

I have been touched by the hand of God and I found the real truth, so now my phone doesn't stop ringing asking me to come speak. The miracle is GOD, not me!

CHAPTER NINETEEN:
HAIRDO RESCUES COMA BOY

One day Faith's mother was helping me with my therapy. She would walk with me down our lane and back up it several times every day. We were about at the end of the lane when we heard someone from the woods around my home yell.

A man came out through the trees with a big smile on his face. He introduced himself to us and we introduced ourselves to him.

We talked for a long time that day. I told him of my fears of leaving my house, and he gained my trust almost immediately.

From that day forward, "Hairdo", his nick-name, made it his goal to get me back into the outside world.

He quickly became my best friend here in West Virginia, and took it upon himself to prove to me that I could do a lot of things the doctors were saying I'd never be able to do again.

For instance, enjoy the outdoors. My passion, other than drugs and drinking before my accident, was spring turkey hunting. There was just something about the sound of a Spring Gobbler gobbling that went straight to my soul.

I really missed hearing that and longed to once again hear a Spring Gobbler…well my buddy was a great Spring Gobbler hunter as well. He could call a turkey like no one I have ever heard before. I was good, but Hairdo was great. He called me one spring morning and was telling me about the huge gobbler he had taken the day before. He then asked me if I had been hearing any early morning gobbles around my house.

That evening God sent me another gift. It was almost dark out on my back porch. I sat with an owl hooter. Any turkey hunter knows that when a gobbler hears an owl he will gobble away his location. Not 30 yards behind my home a gobbler sounds off three times to my owl hooter!

I couldn't wait to call my friend, Hairdo.

After I told Hairdo, he told me to dust off my camo clothing. He would be here at 5am to take me after that bird. After a lot of convincing, Faith talked me into trusting my buddy and God, and I hit the woods once again.

Hairdo put that turkey on my lap that morning. I didn't shoot it. I was just so happy to be able to be back in the spring woods again I didn't care who shot it!

By the way, it wasn't five minutes after my Longbeard turkey walked off that a second Longbeard came running to Hairdo's calls. He took a great 24 pound ten inch gobbler that day.

Thanks, Hairdo, for rescuing me and getting me back to being able to enjoy my turkey hunting passion!

He also took me to work with him. He was a builder and he gave me a job at his building business. My job was to clean up areas where they had been building. He had only two rules for me:

        1) No Power Tools
        2) Stay on the ground

One day after work we stopped to get gas, and sitting in his truck, I kept hearing these words:

"Hey, Coma Boy! Hey, Coma Boy!"

It was the boy who was driving my ATV and caused my accident that day back in 2005! I hadn't seen him since and there he was yelling "Hey, Coma Boy" to *me*!

Now I had a choice to make. Does "Go-Go" get out and do something he's been longing to do since he did this to me, or does David just sit there and pretend he doesn't hear him?

God must have been with me again that day. My tears started falling from my face. I put my head in my hands and shouted, "Shut up!"

I had anger building inside me. If my brothers were there this boy would have met some very unhappy Barrows brothers. But, I now knew that violence would solve nothing.

I let it go and asked God to forgive him for treating me so badly. I don't know what ever became of that boy, but I do know that one day we will all answer for his sins and what goes around comes around.

I have been taught about forgiveness and I know that mean, hateful man I use to be died on May 28th, 2005.

Thanks again, Hairdo!

My friend, Hairdo

Opening Day 2010

Hairdo with his long beard

Hairdo on my mountain ready for work!

CHAPTER TWENTY:
A NEW PURPOSE FOR MY LIFE

After leaving Health South I got bored sitting at home, but God had other plans for me that He was about to put in place, other plans than just keeping me clean and sober. Soon He was going to use me in a way I'd never thought about...

I still felt lost, like I wasn't even in my own body. Mindlessly I followed the direction of my doctor, Bonnie. She introduced me to my psychologist, who I visit still to this day to get direction from.

The local newspaper kept up with my status after the accident, along with the local radio station. The radio station interviewed me on air where I told my whole miracle story from beginning to end.

Suddenly I had TV interviews bombarding me, all wanting my story. Without warning I became the "Hampshire County Miracle Man".

WHAG News 25 from Hagerstown, Maryland contacted me and wanted to do an interview with me, so I did. I talked about the accident, being in a coma and never being able to talk or walk again. I explained how they told me I would need 24 hour care for the rest of my life, and never walk or talk again…

I was told to reach out to others through what is now called my "ATV Safety Miracle Man" talks. I included my T.B.I. (Traumatic brain Injury) story, which has evolved into allowing me to speak out publicly at local schools and organizations about ATV Safety and alcohol and drug abuse.

My own mother told me one day that I could stand and speak to 1,000 people and if only one person heard me it was worth it. God has been such an overpowering voice in my head for me to keep screaming the truth of His power. I will keep speaking and reaching out to anyone and everyone I can and hope this reaches …a still suffering alcoholic or drug addict.

It has been very rewarding to reach out and help others who share similar problems like what cost me my "former" life in my accident in 2005.

I post pictures on Facebook of me talking to all the kids at our local schools and 4-H clubs. Now I am travelling across West Virginia and beyond speaking to schools, giving ATV Safety talks along with drug and alcohol awareness.

I receive standing ovations from almost every school and organization I speak to. There are times I feel so loved and wanted that I allow my ego to say to myself that I am important; I am loved and I do have a Purpose in This Life.

It usually is short-lived, however, when I am back alone to my own thoughts and my Traumatic Brain Injury tells me I am Nothing and Worthless once again.

So, I go, yet again, to my psychologist and family physician and express my thoughts and feelings.

Then, I remind myself that TODAY I SERVE THE GOD who ultimately is in charge of ALL THINGS and who has given me this second chance at this thing called LIFE!

My great friend, Angie, over the phone answers all my doubts and fears in two minutes saying, "David, it's not about you, it's about God, His strength and His power delivering you from your hell here on earth."

Don't get the wrong idea here; I'm not in Hell anymore! I have learned through family, friends and God how to deal with my disabilities.

I love my life today. I have the greatest friends a man could ask for. I have a son who loves his daddy; I'm an uncle who listens and talks to my nieces and nephews; I try to be a son my mom can be proud of; I'm an outspoken member of AA-NA and I'm a man waiting to hear from you to come help save another hurting drug addict, alcoholic or accident victim.

I can be reached by my nickname 8121, which is my telephone number:

304-496-8121, or by my email address:

djbhunts@frontiernet.net

Or, you can see and hear me at any AA or NA meeting anywhere I'm invited to go.

So, yes, I'll continue my speaking because God and Angie and my conscience tell me to…so, in short, I don't know if this will ever help anyone, but it sure helps me.

David with his physician, Bonnie!

My ATV Safety Talks at schools throughout West Virginia…

April, 2011 Edition of The Grapevine – My article

ATV Safety information used at my safety talks…

This is the article that named me "Miracle Man"!

My ATV Safety information I use at my ATV Safety Talks

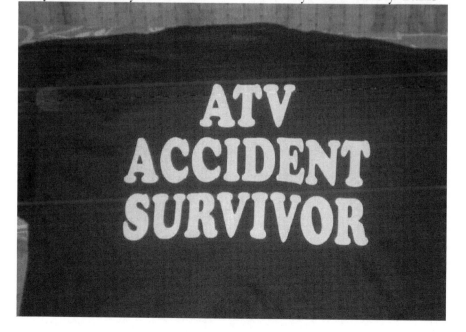

David on his ATV today with proper safety equipment

My son, Hunter, on his Harley with proper safety equipment

Make sure and wear your helmet!

David at one of his school ATV safety talks

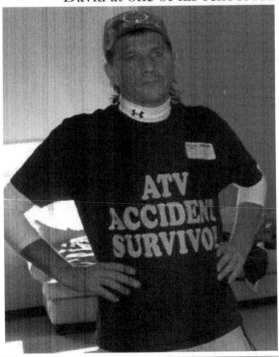

CHAPTER TWENTY-ONE:
MY FRIENDS OLD AND NEW

After returning home from Morgantown Health South Rehab Hospital and getting so much needed help from great friends like Hairdo, Angie, my doctors, therapists and family, I started my new life as David.

I attended as many self-help meetings as I could get to. My life was about to take a drastic change.

I knew, in my heart, I needed to take care of my addictions, so I joined a 12-step program and was given a sponsor. These steps have truly helped me find a way to work through my problems and deal with them in a healthier manner.

I have found and have been helped by Facebook, where I meet many friends and where I can share and reach out to many more that suffer addictions like mine. But, something I didn't know was too much about was my own surroundings where I live.

I never had time to meet my neighbors or any local people here in Hampshire County, West Virginia. I was too busy hiding from them because of my addictions. But now things were going to be different, better!

I first met my ordained minister neighbor who helped me during my accident. He arrived one day at my front door! He had heard I had made it home and wanted to meet me. He was the man who held me in his arms until the paramedics arrived from the Slanesville Fire and Rescue Squad, and here he was on my front porch!

We hugged and talked of God's grace and power. He was an ordained minister and became a great friend. His wife was with him. She had a beautiful voice and sang for me that day as we praised God. It wasn't long after that we stood in front of our whole church and told my story of how God saved a suffering drug addict and alcoholic. There were people crying as they listened to a true story of God's power!

I always wanted to take my son fishing at a local man's pond, but I never had time for him. My previous life was all about finding and using drugs and alcohol.

So, I made the time one day and took my son, Hunter, to the pond near our home and knocked on the door of another neighbor to ask permission to fish. I remember sitting on Junior's porch that day for two hours laughing and talking about my accident.

He was a retired man and has a beautiful wife who, today when I stop, I call 'Mom'. She always has things to give me like blackberry jam or other foods she cans. Hunter and I have caught so many fish at their pond it is crazy. We always put the fish back in, but the memories we share at that pond will live with me forever.

I also met a woman named Leah. She was the first one to get to me the day of my accident. She worked on the EMS crew from Slanesville.

One day my doctor sent me to a local fitness and wellness center to do my physical therapy. My therapist there was Nancy. She and I talked about my accident. Nancy told me there was someone she would like for me to meet the next week. It was her daughter, Leah, who saved my life the first time the day of my wreck.

We sat in a small room that day at the wellness center, just the three of us, as I got the chance to thank them.

I still see her mother now as I am a member of the Health and Fitness Center. She always smiles and asks how I am. Leah's mother has also worked with me in a swimming pool for my therapy.

All kinds of neighbors stop now at my home, wishing me well and asking if I need anything. Where were all these people before my accident? I was so caught up in my world of addiction I never noticed anything or anyone from the time I woke up till the time I passed out... all I was concerned with was killing myself with drugs and drinking.

I am so very grateful God interrupted my life. Today I have an open mind, an open heart, an open door and the greatest friends a man could ask for.

Thank you, Jesus, for sparing my life for the rest of my days here on earth. I will continue to reach out to those who suffer from addiction and alcoholism and lead them to the real truth.

David's home on his mountain

CHAPTER TWENTY-TWO:
ANOTHER TURNING POINT

I was on Facebook one day early on after I returned home from the hospital and I came in contact with Anne LB, a schoolmate of mine. She was in nursing and she talked to me a lot about my problems. I felt comfortable with Anne and she helped me feel comfortable enough to re-join the world.

I told her one day, "One of my biggest regrets is I can't get out. I'm isolated and afraid to join the world again."

She talked me into going to my class reunion AND a KIX concert. I went to her house and spent the night. Her and her husband, Mike, drove me to the Kix concert and I got to meet Brian Forsythe, but the name he goes by is Brian DAMAGE Forsythe, and he is a famous rock star.

It was also the first time that I stepped back into the world since the accident that extended past the safety net of my home community.

…another turning point in my life that I will never forget.

~Thanks, Anne

Anne and David the night before the Kix concert

Brian Forsyth (Kix) and David ("Go-Go") backstage before the show

As I look back now, this was more than just a turning point for me. I was then able to re-join THE WORLD instead of always being scared at my house…it was a Miracle!

Rob "Sal", Anne, David and Barbara at our class reunion

CHAPTER TWENTY-THREE: LEARNING TO LOVE THE "NEW ME"

About a year after returning home from the hospital after the accident, I noticed a lot of things about me that would never be the same. I had Traumatic Brain Damage, or TBI as the doctors called it.

My emotions were like a roller-coaster. My highs were too high and my lows were suicidal lows. There were many days I slept just to pass the time and get away from my own feelings.

I had a lot of time to think… I had lost a great friend to suicide and always wondered if he had made it to Heaven for taking his own life.

Another thing was my son, Hunter. How could I leave him like that? What would he think of me for leaving him like that? Would he ever know how much I loved him? He meant the world to me and my dad wouldn't have ever left me like that!

What about my mom or my brothers who stood beside me for all those years, and mostly what about Faith? How would she go on without her best friend? Did she deserve that from me?

No one would ever understand the pain I have every day. The emotional and physical pain is so intense most days I just want to make it stop.

Faith knew my passion for music and how much I loved listening and pretending to be in the rock band "Def Leppard". They sang lots of songs that related to me, especially, "Two Steps Behind".

They were coming to a venue near us and not telling me, she bought us two very expensive tickets to go see them.

Faith arranged for us to ride in a limousine to the show. I felt like a rock star myself that day, but the biggest fight of all was when, after the show, the drummer, Rick Allen, came from behind his drum set and raised his one arm to the air. It spoke straight to my heart.

This man lost his arm in an auto accident. He struggled like I was struggling, yet he had the courage to find a way to drum again with only one arm.

That day changed my thinking about myself and gave me the courage to go on living and not let my disability stop what God had in store for me.

I am overly grateful for Rick Allen that day. He showed me that there is no mountain too high for God.

I've learned through God not to use drugs or alcohol anymore. I don't need them to change the way I feel or to escape from reality.

I love myself today. I love telling others of my experience in hopes of helping someone else like me. No longer am I "Go-Go" the drug addicted alcoholic who *did find* the three ends as an active user.

How truthful it is in AA and NA when they say there are only three ends to drug addiction. So, go ahead and keep drinking and drugging because I can guarantee you will definitely find these three things at your end:

JAILS ~ INSTITUTIONS ~ DEATH

I was lucky. I was given a second chance so I found ways to make the changes I need to use my life to make sure Hunter has his dad, mom has her son, my brothers have their sibling and Faith has her best friend.

An American Bald Eagle on David's mountain

David, Faith and Hunter backstage at Def Leppard concert

CHAPTER TWENTY-FOUR: MISTAKES ALONG MY JOURNEY

So I start to get some clean time and pats on the back and I start to get back things I've lost; friends, family, possessions and trust. I got angry one evening at a meeting I attended so I think to myself, 'I don't need this crap, I have been clean over two years and I'm not going to be disrespected by anyone, especially someone I'm trying to help'.

I think, 'I'll show you'; I just won't come to this meeting anymore! But who really gets hurt? Am I hurting you by not coming to this certain meeting, or am I hurting myself all over again?

The other person doesn't even know they hurt my feelings; it's not them that have to pay the price. I *will pay* by not getting myself to this meeting. I don't want to go back to jail; I don't want to be placed in a mental ward. And, I certainly I don't wanna die!

So I call my sponsor and other friends to vent. I learn about my ego, and find out what my ego really means:

Easing ~ God ~ Out

So, I go to a mirror in my home and look at myself. Who am I looking at? Is this "Go-Go" or is this David? Just that fast I realize that my addiction has snuck in and taken over my thinking, AGAIN! My disease is cunning, baffling and powerful. I go to the one thing I know will save me from myself; God.

I make any amends I need to make and get through another day being clean and sober. By not getting involved in my new way of life, I'm only challenging my disease or addiction. So, I get involved, very involved.

I started my own Saturday night meeting. I go to the prison every Friday night at 7pm. I do the Juvenile Detention Center talk every chance I get. I'm a speaker at many meetings. I sponsor other recovering addicts. I make coffee; I clean ashtrays and set up chairs. Does this sound fun to you? Well it's kept me clean for over ten years now, so it must work.

Another lesson I've learned the hard way is people, places and things.

Do I belong in a bar? Do I hang out with people who use drugs or alcohol? Should I have needles and other drug paraphernalia around me? NO...

It's just that simple. If I hang around a dirty dog, I'm gonna get fleas.

My "Go-Go" days are over. There are a lot of young pretty women who come to our meetings. I've learned that under every skirt is a slip, so as far as I'm concerned the ladies help the ladies and the men help the men.

Yes, I have great women friends today, but that's as far as it goes for me... they are friends. "Go-Go" is GONE!

I'd like to forget my past, but God gave me a daily reminder with my reconstructed face, daily pain and the loss of sight in my left eye. I only have one eye today, but I see clearer than I've ever seen.

Anger and resentments have almost taken me out, so I've learned to let go and let God today.

One day a neighbor had some work he needed done and asked me to help. I agreed and he picked me up at 8am the next morning. Driving to another neighbor's home, he pulled a baggie of marijuana out and began to smoke it. Not knowing how to react at that moment I thought of real friends and would they do this to me?

On one hand, I have this one boy offering me pot. He was telling me how good it was as he handed me the bowl. This was the first time since my accident that drugs had been offered to me.

On the other hand, I had a whole new set of friends who I know would not understand why I relapsed on a drug I didn't even ever care for.

So, it was decision time. Do I smoke the pot or not? We were ten miles from my home but at that moment I didn't care if I were in another country… I asked him to pull over NOW!

Handing him back his bowl, I got out of his truck telling him to leave me there or I was calling the cops. I walked for two miles crying, hoping no one would notice me along the road. Well, no one did as I walked the whole ten miles back to my home. The walk about killed me, cars travelling fast driving right by me. But, I knew I made the right choice.

I made it home and called my sponsor. We talked for an hour. I listened intently to him tell me about lessons learned and who my REAL friends really are!

CHAPTER TWENTY-FIVE:
LEAVE BAR TALK AT THE BAR

One night at an AA meeting I was so pumped up about the topic I couldn't wait to share. They were talking about gratitude, and I was given a second chance at life. I had a lot to be grateful for.

First, I spoke of my sons Bradley and Hunter; how I was grateful to be back in Brad's life. Although he now lived in Tennessee with his mother and her husband, they have allowed me to call and keep in touch with him.

David with sons Hunter and Bradley

Then I spoke of Hunter. How today I can be his father and best friend. I cried as I talked about how God had answered my prayers and how these meetings kept me grounded each day. I got so caught up in the moment, I used language you normally only hear at a bar.

Bad curse words came out of my mouth and I noticed my sponsor no longer looking at me as I shared. The meeting ended and afterward he asked to speak to me alone. He started the conversation by saying he loved me which meant Ohh… Man, he was about to tell me something I didn't like.

He said now that I had some clean and sober time, I needed to work on my language. He said my language belonged in a bar and we weren't in a bar. Not knowing what to say to him, I told him I would ask God to help me. I love my sponsor, but he is straight to the point with me; no beating around the bushes. His recovery is his life and nothing comes between him and his God.

I love that about him. I can't tell you how many times I've asked him for his 40 years clean time with the same answer each time. He would say no, I have to earn it!

I find myself talking with one of my brothers or friends today and, when I swear, it just sounds wrong, so God must still be working in my life. What an awesome God I serve today, never leaving me and walking with me on this road of life I'm on.

CHAPTER TWENTY-SIX:
MORE GIFTS IN RECOVERY

I love to speak. I wanna be heard. I'm very outspoken and I have proof of my message. I go to the Juvenile Detention Center here in my hometown. I tell the kids there is a way out of trouble. I tell my story and how God touched my life and He is waiting for them to give their lives to Him as well. I am not a pulpit pounding preacher; I am a true real life miracle of God's sent to help others get to the truth which is God.

I'm not a very spiritual man, but if asked where I stand on religion I say I stand with the truth, the Holy Bible and my friends and family.

Other gifts I have received have to start with my son, Hunter. I'm his dad, his playmate, his friend, his teacher and his clean and sober buddy.

There have been times during my hospital stay I wanted to be dead. I hated how my face looked and how my brain doesn't work now. If it hadn't been for my son, Hunter, and being back in touch with my first son, Bradley I would have killed myself. But my dad wouldn't have done that to me, so I fought off my demons, and as I learned in recovery…this too shall pass!

David and Bradley at Penn National

Hunter and David at the beach

I have a support group today. People I call when I'm down and also when I'm having a good day; Carol, Cindy, Mike, Keith, Marvin, Karen, Gene and many others who will talk with me, day or night, about life's problems. I also have all six of my brothers back; Johnny, Alan, Jeff, Mark, Kevin, Jimmy; we are once again the Barrows boys…

I have regained my friendships with so many of my dearest friends, Rob B., Rob S., Anne LB, and many more who now trust me and believe in me. It's amazing to me how God has worked in my life. I also got back in touch with my first wife, Luanne, who went on to have two beautiful children of her own. Other gifts I have been given is this amazing willpower to reach out to others who suffer from addiction. My life now belongs to God and I follow His rules.

TAKE GOD OUT OF THE PICTURE AND WHAT ARE YOU LEFT WITH…YOUR DEMONS TO DEAL WITH ALONE!

I have to remember where I came from. I'm reminded of that at local meetings I go to when a newcomer comes in suffering from this disease I have. I listen with all my heart when someone comes in and reminds me that the drugs and alcohol are still out there waiting for me. I see the pain and hear the stories of how addiction is killing people; my best friend growing up is dead today because of a heroin overdose.

Another great friend put a gun in his mouth and pulled the trigger after stealing all his family's guns and possessions and selling them for crack cocaine. I have been to funerals of loved ones I've lost to drunken driving car accidents.

Just recently Faith and I buried her best friend, Peanut, because she chose to drink and drive. Did all these people have God in their lives? I don't know, but my family, friends and life mean more to me than any drink or drug ever did. God has led me to write this book, and I will not be quiet any longer about the effects of alcohol and drug addiction. I have been saved by the grace of God, and until I'm called home with Him, I will continue to reach out to others screaming:

THERE IS A WAY OUT!

His name is Jesus Christ. Just ask Him for His help and allow Him to lead you

CHAPTER TWENTY-SEVEN: WHAT I DO WITH ANGER AND HURT TODAY

I've learned I don't hurt well. When my feelings get hurt I use to cover the pain with alcohol and drugs. It was better than feeling all those emotions. I was a Barrows boy; we didn't cry!

I didn't want to be looked at or thought of as a sissy, so I buried the pain, pretended it didn't bother me and drunk and drugged it away, hoping it would never come back. But, reality really hit me when my mind altering drink or drug wore off.

Now it was worse than when it started. Now I had remorse to add to my feelings. It's no wonder I tried killing myself three times before my God interrupted my miserable life and gave me a free gift of my accident, May 28, 2005.

Yes, I'm human, yes I still get angry and hurt today, but I've learned to live life on life's terms. I'm not in charge, I'm not the boss and I'm not the man I thought I was. I'm merely a man that God gave a second chance at life and I plan on taking full advantage of it!

I've learned to talk about my hurt today; it was a huge wall I had built to protect myself from. Back then I hated a mirror, it reflected the truth and I couldn't face that, a drug addicted alcoholic who hated himself and others.

I couldn't stand to be with any one person too long for fear they might see David, who wasn't who I wanted others to see. I wanted them to see this very cool, good looking, smarter than them, man. In reality I was only fooling myself… people now tell me who they saw was a lying, deceitful, struggling drug addict who wanted no help, only to use or drink again.

I hid from David very well. He only came out when "Go-Go" was so low and desperate that he figured David could save him, through tears and showing his real emotions, until someone felt bad for me and reached for my hand to help.

It was a mechanism I used so many times to get "Go-Go" out of the trouble he created. It worked almost every time.

I went to four different rehabs, lots of hospitals and spent many nights at friends' homes because they felt sorry for me because I had nowhere else to go.

Today I look back and think of those who helped me; my dad, my mom, my brothers, my first two wives, my first sponsor, Bob, all the counselors at the rehabs and Mary, an alcohol and drug counselor in Gettysburg, Pennsylvania.

I wish I could find Mary today; I'd love to show her David! She tried so hard to help me and we really got along. The only problem was that "Go-Go" wasn't going to let anybody interfere with what he had in mind, which was death to David. And, until "Go-Go" met his match (God), was anyone going to stop him?

I learned with the power and strength of my God, it didn't matter what I had done or even who I thought I was. He knew what was in my heart. He also knew I loved Him, but there were demons dragging me away from Him. He let it go for a long time until I would drop to my knees one lonely night and beg Him for forgiveness, asking Him to please come save me from myself!

Today I drop to my knees every chance I get to pray and wherever He leads me I will follow.

CHAPTER TWENTY-EIGHT: THIS IS ABOUT WE…NOT ME!

After finding my way back to recovery and choosing my now best friend and sponsor, Rich, I attended as many AA and NA recovery program meetings as I could get to. I found there were many meetings in my local area and I met many others who suffered from the disease of alcohol and drug addiction.

I learned a new way to live. When I first was able to speak and share my story, I thought no one could ever possibly understand that every day when I awoke the first thought was to drink and do drugs. I remember now how many people I had hurt just trying to get to my drink or drug. But, it was a story they had heard before or lived themselves. I was merely another person living with this disease.

If I wanted to find help all I needed was to just show up and listen, so I did. At that point in my life I was willing to do anything to stop this insane way of living. So, I turned my will and my life over to the care of God, and asked Him to guide me in this thing called recovery. It was and still is very hard getting out of my own way.

First, I had to be honest, and for so long all I knew was to be a liar and a thief. Next, I had to be open minded, that meant to be open to suggestions. Did they mean I had to do things their way? No, it only meant I had to think about what they had found that works for them. Then I had to be willing. Well, I had tried everything else on my own to stay sober and none of it ever worked.

I ended up in jails, in institutions, and I even found death! So, yes I was willing to find a new way of living.

This was not a ME program, it was a WE thing. I can't, but we can! I learned that with God all things are possible!

They told me I'd never walk or talk ever again after my accident, and today I'm not only walking, but you can't shut me up when I speak about my God's power. He took a drug addicted, alcoholic that was suicidal and a threat to society and changed me into a vessel for Him. Today I'm clean and sober only because of Him, my sponsor and a few friends.

I'm a father to my sons, Bradley and Hunter. I'm a brother to my six brothers, a son to my mother, a sponsor to other suffering addicts and a true friend. I'm trustworthy and loyal, and always tell the truth today...but mostly, I'm happy with the man in the mirror that God saved to help save others.

David today, on his mountain, praising his God

CHAPTER TWENTY-NINE:
A LESSON IN EGO

My ego got me in so much trouble through my life. I thought because I had money or came from a big family I could get away with anything. I bought my way out of jail before; I paid others to like me. For instance, I took people into expensive stores and let them buy anything they wanted so they would think I liked them, or I would buy expensive gifts for people that I hardly knew.

My ego grew so big that I looked down on others thinking I was better than them. I lost many friends because I wouldn't hang out with them because they didn't have what I had; a nice vehicle, money or a job like mine.

I thought because my brothers were good at things then that must mean I was good at them too. My oldest brother, Johnny, was a track and field star. He also was semi-pro football player. My brother, Alan, was the common sense brother and ran my father's business. My brother, Jeff, went into the Army and became a guard at a huge army depot in Chambersburg, PA. My brother, Kevin, was not only the best looking Barrows boy, and he worked for the PA Turnpike making plenty of money. My youngest brother, Jimmy, was a little bit of all of us and became my rock of brotherhood standing beside me when I fell in 2005.

My ego cost me all of them. I thought I could beat addiction; and I did, but only by learning the hard way.
There are three ways out of active addiction; jails, institutions and death.

Well I did find all three of those, and only by the grace of God today I have all my brothers back. I will be forever grateful for that. One of my sponsors in recovery once told me what ego meant: E G O = Easing God Out

Today I try and control EGO and the rewards are well worth all I had to go through to get it all figured out!

Brothers Mark and Alan with David

I now have back my family, my faith and my friends!

Life is GOOD!

CHAPTER THIRTY:
REACHING OUT AND HELPING
OTHER BOTTOMS

I was told by an old friend I use to know to stop living in the past. She told me I sounded like a cry baby always talking about my accident and my "Go-Go" days.

If it wasn't for my "Go-Go" days and my true testimony I wouldn't have a story to tell. I would just be another face in the crowd and another person who died from drug abuse and alcoholism.

I have lost three great friends to addiction and I died myself on May 28, 2005. I feel my friends screaming at me to save myself and others.

I'm known where I live as a very outspoken person when it comes to recovery and telling the truth about addiction.

Reaching my hand out helps me the most by being the face of recovery for other sufferers. I'm a very happy grateful recovering drug addict and alcoholic and am asked to speak all over my state of West Virginia.

I've stood in front of 1500 people crying when I tell of God's strength and power. I'm in many newspaper articles about my recovery and its' miracles.

What helps me each day is to know I'm not alone. I have an unstoppable God, a one-of-a-kind sponsor, and the greatest friends a man could ask for when another struggling addict or alcoholic is hurting.

That's when David really comes out. I can not only feel their pain, but I can show them this way of life was God's answer to my desperate prayer of 'please save me from this disease of addiction'.

I live my life for others today. It's not about me anymore; it's a WE thing. I came from death to saving lives and no one is going to stop me from reaching my hand out to help.

Someone was there when I was bottoming, and I will be there when they bottom too. I'm not a miracle; I'm just a man that God has used to show others the truth.

At my prison meeting, the convicts have named my Friday night meetings the "Circle of Truth"! One Friday evening I asked if I was helping anyone. The whole room full of convicts, one after another, told me that if it wasn't for my truth and my testimony they wouldn't come or have any hope for their future.

But each one of them knows that I have come and spoke so they can see a light at the end of their tunnel.

I will scream at the top of my lungs: "There IS a way out! Together we stand, divided we fall. It's not about me, it's about WE!"

One day at a time I will love my life clean and sober. The gifts I've received are too numerous to mention, but, I like me today. I will help you today. I am a son, a brother, a friend and a father all because I was willing to take advice from someone who had been there and done that, and God saved my life!

Faith and my son, Hunter, today

CHAPTER THIRTY-ONE: HOW I STOPPED THE INSANITY (HELP IS ON THE WAY)

So many people I have talked to have told me it's inappropriate to talk about drug and alcohol related suicide and the families who are survived by them. I disagree.

My family had given up on me, trying everything they could think of, but none of it was enough for me to stop.

I had been to four different rehabilitations centers. I had been to prison and I moved away from my family too numerous places thinking it was the area I lived in that kept me using drugs and drinking. What I found out was everywhere I moved the drug addict and alcoholic followed me.

From time to time I would call back home and speak to my mother, dad and brothers, but I knew in my heart I was not welcomed as long as I was still in the grip of my addictions. I remember crying a lot after calling home. I missed my family so much, but by now the first thought each day as I awoke was how I will get drugs or money to buy drugs or alcohol today.

I remember thinking there is no hope or help for me. This was going to be the way I would die, either from overdosing on drugs or an accident from drinking too much.

Well that's exactly what happened to two great friends growing up! One died from a drug overdose and the other one killed himself after a night of using and drinking. I didn't want that to happen to me.

I was too smart to let drugs and drinking kill me, or so I thought.

I went to my friend's funeral after he committed suicide. I sat with his mother who was so broken I felt she would never mend from her loss.

She put her arm around me that day and asked, "David, what is it about those drugs that killed my son?"

How could I answer this woman? The truth would tear her heart out, so I just hugged her and asked God to be with this struggling family.

The truth is alcohol and drugs are very cunning, baffling and extremely powerful; and, if not arrested, they will kill eventually, EVERY TIME, no matter how smart you think you are…

What I mean by arrested is this. Alcohol and drugs cannot just be put down and stopped by an alcoholic or addict. Addicts or alcoholics can fool us or others by saying:

"I can stop anytime I want to."

But, by not using or drinking for short periods of time, it can be followed by short bursts of relapsing which has killed so many.

The truth is I'm grateful to have found the world's greatest friends in AA – NA.

I go to more meetings than any one man could go. I go to the juvenile detention centers. I go to prison meetings. I attend my weekly area meetings. I have a sponsor who understands me. I pray constantly all day if I have to. I have a phone list of over 100 other recovering people. I speak when asked, which I get to do a lot, but I want more. I want what my sponsor has; over 40 years of recovery and a wonderful life!

I have asked my sponsor for the happiness that he has. I've told him I want what he has and his reply is always the same:

"David, I won't give you what I have. I had to work for it, but I can show you how to get it. Now, get to work!"

Today I sponsor others in recovery. I have the greatest friends ever and it gives me such pride and joy.
I can't wait for my phone to ring; being asked to come share my story. I have my family back today! I have all six of my brothers and my mother, the saint. I get to go visit my dad's grave now with a clear conscience, and I know he is in Heaven saving a spot for me.

What a wonderful life I have found in recovery. What a powerful God I serve today. What helps me the most is helping another alcoholic or addict to not drink or use…just for today! My God is an awesome God and He loves you too!

Front row L to R: Mark, Barbara (MOM) and Jimmy
Back row L to R: Jeff, Alan, Kevin and David (ME)

CHAPTER THRITY-TWO:
IS THIS HELPING ANYONE?

As I sit home thinking, all my doubts and fears enter my brain-damaged mind…does anyone really care about MY life? Will I save anybody the horrifying life I lived as an acoholic and drug addict? Will anyone read between the lines and think maybe it's my drinking and drug use that has caused my life to be so messed up?

Well, one thing is for sure, if you continue to use or drink, trust me when I say this…It will get WORSE!

I'm just trying to scream at the top of my lungs:

"THERE IS A WAY OUT!"

Like I said before, my own mother told me one day that I could stand and speak to 1,000 people and if only one person heard me, it was worth it.

God has been such an overpowering voice in my head for me to keep screaming the truth of His power. I will keep writing this hoping it reaches you!

CHAPTER THIRTY-THREE:
TAKE THE 'T' OUT OF CAN'T AND TOGETHER WE CAN!

Today my life is so different from the life I lived before my miracle. I no longer guess God's will for me. I have learned first-hand that this thing we call life and living is not controlled by "Go-Go", or even David, as much as my ego (Easing God Out) would like to think, or that I'm that important... I'm just one more warrior of His who was given a second chance to live!

I'm surrounded now by my family and great friends. Not long ago they received a phone call to come say goodbye to their drug addicted, alcoholic who pushed as far and as hard as he could to find his way out, only to find that death was at the end of that road.

I'm clean and sober over 10 years now with a list as long as this book of those who helped me. Most importantly, I learned the hard way that all I needed to do was surrender my will and life over to the care of my unstoppable God. I'm happy to say, we have the greatest friendship any two people can have!

He has given me back all the things I lost through addiction and alcoholism, and so much more; my mom, my six brothers, my sons, my best friends Rob B. and Rob S., Tracy, Micah, Angie, my sponsor, Hairdo, Faith and so many more. But mostly, He gave me back the relationship I lost with Him when I selfishly chose a drug and drink over Him.

I've been given so many gifts since my 'miracle accident'. Some days I just sit and smile and wonder how I ever went from a suicidal man to one who treasures every step and breathe that is given each new day!

I now travel across the country giving ATV safety talks, drug and alcohol awareness speeches, motivational and inspirational talks, and the Miracle Man story to schools, clubs, organizations, churches, wherever I'm invited to speak.

After every talk I give now I'm surrounded by people who look up to me and respect me for what I am doing…saving lives through my own experiences.

Living and dealing with my T.B.I. has been my greatest challenge so far. I have to surround myself with positive people and positive sayings like the one Tracy Rice taught me after my accident.

"Take the 'T' out of the word can't, David, and together WE CAN do this."

I have my moments of anger, resentments, fear, hatred, but no longer do I hold on to those negative self-destructing thoughts. Life is too short and precious to waste time on these feelings and thoughts…live, laugh, love is what I say now when I'm lost or confused.

My doctor, Bonnie, has not only walked this road with me for many years now, but has given me a friendship not many have with a physician. She helps take away my physical daily pain I still suffer in my face, back and chest, and she has also led me back to my God.

"See you in church on Sunday, David!" she will say after every visit.

Sharing my true story not only helps me realize that this did happen to me, but reaching others who are T.B.I. survivors lets me know I'm not alone in this.

There are many, many others just like me and we are strong. We are survivors, and there is hope for a brighter future. There is strength in numbers.

I have started a new T.B.I. support group in my hometown, and I am loved and cared for by others who are just like me. Some days I don't think I deserve that gift, but I am reassured during my meetings and through my Facebook family I am…and, so are they!

This story needed to be told, not for me but for you, the reader, who may be caught up in or hiding from an invisible disease of alcoholism, drug addiction or T.B.I... there is an answer, there is hope and there is a future! We only have to believe and trust others who are travelling down the same road as us.

It's a WE thing I've learned. I am not alone anymore. No more running, no more hiding; let the truth be told and allow God to lead the way to the kind of life I always wanted...happy, joyous and free!

And, as Alligator Angie and I say before we hang up the phone....Jesus loves you!

Remember to take the 'T' out of can't so WE CAN!

ABOUT THE WRITERS

Melodye Faith Hathaway is a free-lance writer, motivational speaker on loss, grief and inspiration, poet/author publisher. She writes and Blogs for many on-line publications and has published several E-books and paperbacks including her most recent "In Search of Jeremy" and "The Lightning Bug Named Blue".

She lives in Hiawatha, Kansas with her husband, Roger. She enjoys making handcrafted beaded bookmarks to go along with the books she writes, and helping others get their stories out. Her email is: melodye.hathaway@gmail.com

She met David Barrows through a mutual motivational speaker, but the two have never met in person. This book was written totally by emails, phone calls, texts and Facebook communications.

David Barrows is a motivational speaker who speaks across the country to schools and organizations about ATV Safety, alcoholism, drugs and T.B.I.

He lives in Augusta, West Virginia with his fiancé, Faith Kranenberg, and their son, Hunter Jacob.

Hearing a turkey gobble in the spring is what David lives for. He is an avid Spring Gobbler hunter where he travels from Missouri to West Virginia chasing wild turkeys each year.

One of the most important aspects in his life is to maintain his sobriety. David's email is: djbhunts@frontiernet.net

29102021R00110

Made in the USA
Middletown, DE
07 February 2016